BRITISH
BUILDING
FIRSTS

BRITISH BUILDING FIRSTS
A FIELD GUIDE
DAVID CRAWFORD

DAVID & CHARLES
Newton Abbot   London

For Elizabeth

British Library Cataloguing in Publication Data

Crawford, David
  British building firsts.
  1. Great Britain. Buildings. Architectural features
  I. Title
  720'.941

  ISBN 0-7153-9271-9

Printed in Great Britain
by Butler & Tanner   Frome and London
for David & Charles Publishers plc
Brunel House   Newton Abbot   Devon

CONTENTS

AUTHOR'S PREFACE

This book aims to fill a gap of which I first became aware in 1975 when invited to write a companion book to the heritage walks which the City of London Corporation had laid out to mark European Heritage Year. In undertaking the necessary research I was intrigued to discover how many of the earliest purpose-designed office buildings in Britain still existed. In 1978 an article commissioned by Victor Keegan of *The Guardian* gave me the opportunity to develop my findings on offices and further investigation soon suggested that a good many more building firsts (some of them world as well as British) could be identified and, in many cases, still seen or visited today. With oldest survivors added, I could hypothesise a 'museum' whose exhibits stood in all corners of the British Isles from Kent to the Scottish islands, from Bristol to Edinburgh and from Dublin to Lincolnshire.

Since nobody seemed to have catalogued them all it seemed a good excuse for a book and I am grateful to my agent, Jane Conway-Gordon, for placing it and to David & Charles for agreeing to publish it. I have treated each building type as the subject for a short reference essay, describing the pioneer building or oldest survivor in context and then taking the story on as far as seems relevant historically and geographically. Some subjects have been well researched, and I have relied heavily on the people and sources named in the acknowledgements and bibliography. Others still await definitive treatments and I hope that this slim volume may inspire scholars with more time than I have to give them due justice. Finally, architectural history, archaeology and industrial archaeology are all live disciplines with new discoveries continually being made. I hope to be able to take account of any which are relevant in future editions.

David Crawford
Bickley, Kent

INTRODUCTION

The story of the origin and development of distinct kinds of buildings is summed up very succinctly by Sir Nikolaus Pevsner in his *History of Building Types*, as 'diversification following function'. Medieval British society in fact needed relatively few variations on the basic theme of accommodation, because its separate functional requirements were few and could be housed in a handful of building types. Economic activity, including production and trade, was essentially based on the house of the craftsman or merchant, the family homestead or farmstead — and this domestic tradition continues to this day, in agriculture. Only in the eighteenth century did industrial technology finally outgrow the domestic setting and require unmistakably dedicated structures; in commerce, the practice of the merchant living above his shop endured into the Victorian age.

The need to worship was the earliest human practice which required separate accommodation outside the home environment, and Britain is well endowed with evidence of both pre-Christian and early Christian religious activity. The Church was the single most important building organisation during the Middle Ages, producing thousands of churches, cathedrals, abbeys and monasteries whose concerns extended well beyond liturgical needs, and created a complete social and educational infrastructure — it was the Church which provided the first post-Roman schools, libraries and hospitals in Britain. 'Hospital' was a more general term then than now, given the primitive state of contemporary medical knowledge, and the role of caring for the needy rather than specifically curing the sick anticipated the modern welfare state. The needy also included travellers and pilgrims, who would seek shelter in the guest house of a religious community when inns were few and far between. Abbeys and monasteries were also important centres of agricultural and industrial production. London's Covent Garden market was originally a smallholding of Westminster Abbey; while the twelfth-century Bordesley Abbey in Hereford and Worcester contributed to the west Midlands region's later pre-eminence in metal manufacture.

The business of government was initally carried on in and from the houses of kings, and of the lords (both spiritual and temporal) who were their advisers and territorial representatives under the feudal system. Parliament and the courts sat in the king's palace; barons dispensed local justice in their halls; and the civil service originated in the town houses of the king's ministers. The Norman Conquest brought important innovative buildings which were designed to symbolise and reinforce the exercise of authority: the castle and the public government building (as Westminster Hall). These were built in stone to emphasise the permanence of the new régime and to inspire awe in the subject population; the original timber castles were soon rebuilt in masonry, as were the new cathedrals and abbeys which the Normans erected to replace the often humbler Anglo-Saxon structures.

Versatile as well as durable, castles survived the loss of their military significance to fulfil a variety of civil uses — from prisons to museums — which in some cases have lasted until today; no other type of building has ever been as dramatically expressive of its rôle in the history of Britain. With the passage of centuries, government — by consent rather than force — developed in complexity, initially taking over the sites and structures of abandoned palaces until the need for buildings dedicated to its own particular use became inescapable. Local government, which at first barely existed outside London, took longer to develop and in its present form, is one of the lasting monuments to the Victorian sequence of reforms.

Most of the building types described in the pages which follow are comparatively modern, their arrival on the scene serving to emphasise the quickening pace of social, cultural and commercial activity over the last three centuries. Some — like the libraries and museums which are now a focal point for every civilised community, or the power stations and telephone exchanges which keep modern society working — began their eventful histories as little more than rooms or basements. Others — like shopping arcades, exhibition centres and (in the present century) sports halls — arrived to meet emergent needs brand new, constructed in newly available building materials.

MATERIALS

In the Middle Ages most buildings were of earth or timber. Stone stood for wealth and authority, which is why the Normans made such good use of it in their unprecedented building programmes; while brick, which had been well used by the Romans, had relatively humble connotations until Tudor times. Timber continued to be widely used in domestic building until the seventeenth century when, following the Great Fire of London, the authorities revised and improved building and material standards so as to limit the scale of any future conflagration. From then on, Britain was rebuilt in stone and brick.

The Industrial Revolution introduced the 'iron age' of building design and construction. Iron could now be produced in serviceable strengths and quantities for the erection of the fireproof and large-span structures needed for industrial production on the grand scale. Glass could also now be produced in economical sizes and had been freed from previously prohibitive taxes, and together, these two made possible a whole new generation of commercial buildings — arcades, covered markets and exhibition halls.

The 'iron age' was followed by that of steel. Structural steel or steel-reinforced concrete frames characterise the constructional methods used for large buildings in the twentieth century; these are then clad in stone, brick, glass, metal or composite panelling depending on aesthetic or budgetary demands.

AIRPORTS

Unlike the railways in the previous century, air travel was slow to acquire purpose-designed buildings. One reason was that its development was interrupted by two world wars — which, while stimulating aircraft production and providing good training for future civil pilots, inhibited international travel. Another was the much smaller number of people carried; not until after World War II did air travel become a means of mass transportation.

The world's first regular scheduled international air service left London for Paris (Le Bourget) on 25 August 1919, sixteen years after Orville Wright had made his pioneering flight at Kitty Hawk, North Carolina, USA. It carried a single passenger, mail and papers, and several brace of grouse, and took off from a grass field at a military aerodrome at Hounslow Heath, 26km (16 miles) west of London, where former hangars were used as the terminal. The following year the War Office reclaimed Hounslow Heath, and Croydon aerodrome, which lay a similar distance to the south of London, was adopted as Britain's first official civil airport. Five years earlier the site had been New Barn Farm, a stretch of good wheat-growing Surrey farmland; but in December 1915, with World War I raging and the air a battleground for the first time in history, it had been requisitioned by the Royal Flying Corps (a predecessor of the Royal Air Force) to help in the defence of London.

Croydon was better equipped for civilian use than Hounslow Heath, although for its first seven years of operation (1920–7) the airline companies were obliged to make do with the temporary timber buildings put up for the Corps. The airport hotel was the first in the country to provide air travellers with meals and accommodation, and was only able to open for business in its bungalow-like premises after a prolonged battle with the local licensing magistrates and aggrieved hoteliers, who wanted to know why the previous military canteen was inadequate. A very modest affair, the aerodrome was compared by Harper, Harry and Brenard (see Bibliography) to 'a wild-west township of the early mining days'. But even so, Croydon was in advance of its American counterparts: Atlanta opened in 1925 but only as a single hangar in a field, and it was not until 1927 with the opening of Dearborn, Michigan, that the USA had an airport worthy of the name.

Air travel developed steadily in peacetime conditions, and in 1926 work began on replacing Croydon's inherited buildings with the world's first purpose-built international airport. Designed by Air Ministry architects, this opened in 1928 immediately to the east of the original aerodrome. The centrepiece of the new Croydon was the two-storey terminal building facing the London to Brighton

9

Plate 1 The main entrance to Croydon Airport when still in use as an air terminal. *(Heritage Division, London Borough of Sutton Leisure Services)*

road, dominated at the rear by a 15.25m (50ft) high control tower with its control room surrounded by a continuous observation balcony and rising over three storeys of offices (a design which reappeared in other airports, including Moscow's). The internal planning was a microcosm of future airport development. Passengers entered a spacious concourse surrounded by airline offices; beyond this lay passport controls and the customs hall; and from here a corridor ran round the base of the control tower to the departure gate. The upper floor was devoted to offices for airlines and airport administration. Outside there were no paved runways — planes took off from and landed on turf, using the whole field to manoeuvre in according to wind conditions and relying on marker lines and lights in the grass.

As the gateway to a new dimension, Croydon Airport was surprisingly stolid in architectural treatment. Its functional, reinforced concrete structure was dressed up with heavy motifs — rustication, arched windows and pilasters which appeared to be in stone but were in fact of cement aggregate, and altogether reminiscent of a provincial railway station. The result betrays its bureaucratic origins in its revealing contrast with the nineteenth-century treatment of the great rail termini by the entrepreneurial railway companies and their designers; subsequent airports built over the next decade, with their smooth concrete finishes, reflected the more modernistic 1930s idiom. But Croydon enjoyed both prestige and drama; it was from here, in 1930, that Amy Johnson took off on her epic solo flight to Australia, as recorded on a plaque in the new airport hotel which was built at the same time to replace the bungalow.

With a break for military service during World War II, Croydon continued to function as a civil airport until 1959, by which time the operational requirements of larger, more powerful passenger aircraft had made closure inevitable. London had spread too tightly round suburban Croydon to allow room for expansion and Gatwick, 50km (31 miles) from London, out in the country, had been developing to the point where it could meet the need for an airport to the south of London. The site of the original (ex-Royal Flying Corps) Croydon aerodrome is now the Roundshaw housing estate, designed by Clifford Culpin & Partners in the 1960s. The streets enshrine the rôle played by the area in the history of civil aviation, with names commemorating aircraft makes and manufacturers (Roe Way, Brabazon Avenue, De Havilland Road); aviators (Alcock Close, Lindbergh Road); and the early carriers (Instone Close, Daimler Way). The terminal of the 1928 Croydon Airport is listed for preservation because of its historic interest and survives as Airport House, now an office building on the industrial estate subsequently developed. There are plans for restoring the building and converting the control tower into a museum of air travel; these were under discussion as this book went to press.

GATWICK

The oldest surviving operational airport building in Britain is the original terminal at Gatwick, known as the 'Beehive' because of its pioneering circular plan and now used as administrative offices. Gatwick began life in 1930 as a licensed

Plate 2 The 'Beehive' building at Gatwick Airport in its early days. *(John King)*

private aerodrome on a field next to Gatwick racecourse on the Surrey/Sussex border. Its key advantage with regard to future commercial development was that it lay immediately alongside the main railway line from Brighton to London, offering the prospect of fast connections with the capital. In March 1934 the airport acquired the public licence necessary for it to operate commercial flights, and official acknowledgement of its suitability for development — initially as a relief for Croydon. A few months later the 'father of Gatwick Airport', Morris Jackaman, conceived the inspired idea of building a circular terminal — the first in the world — which he thought would increase the manoeuvrability of aircraft on the ground.

The terminal, complete with telescopic gangways for covered access, was completed in 1936. Its architects had won a competition to turn Jackaman's vision into reality, and were the specially formed partnership of Hoar, Marlow & Lovett, with Alan Marlow as the partner principally in charge. Their brief was that, as well as being circular, the building should be low and white for easy aerial recognition. As built by Jackaman's family firm, it rose in height from a single storey at the outer perimeter to the four-storey control tower at the heart. The central core was of reinforced concrete construction based on two circular ring beams; the outer portion had a structural steel frame with brick infilling to allow for future expansion. A tunnel gave passengers direct access to trains.

Gatwick represented a considerable advance on Croydon, although it was not until the 1950s that the next circular terminal was built (in North America). After spending World War II under military control, it emerged as the prime candidate for Britain's second main civil airport after Heathrow. A new development programme began in 1955 and three years later Queen Elizabeth II opened Gatwick's new terminal — the first in the world to be integrated with a railway station. In 1983, with passenger traffic rising rapidly, the terminal was extended by a circular satellite (the first reprise of Jackaman's vision in Britain for nearly fifty years) and the two are connected by an unmanned train; a completely new north terminal followed in 1988. Gatwick is now the world's third busiest international passenger airport.

HEATHROW

With the end of hostilities in World War II the search began for a new location for Britain's major international airport, as near as possible to the centre of London and with sufficient land to meet the anticipated future demand for air travel. The choice eventually fell on an area of Hounslow Heath which had been in use as an RAF transport depot since 1943, and which had early associations with civil aviation — the site of the London end of the original London to Paris air service lies buried under one of the runways. Heathrow was developed as a star-shaped pattern of runways based on those used by the RAF, with administration and passenger accommodation at the centre — when the airport first opened in 1946 this was primitive in the extreme, with tents for passengers and caravans for airport administration. It was only in 1950 that the government commissioned Sir Frederick Gibberd to design the first permanent central terminal, which opened in 1955.

Heathrow is now the world's busiest international airport. Each year it handles nearly 300,000 air traffic movements, some 35 million passengers (more than any airport outside the USA) and over 600,000 tonnes of mail and cargo. It has expanded steadily to meet rising demand, with new terminals or terminal extensions opening in 1961, 1968, 1970 and (most recently) 1986, when Terminal 4 became operational to the south of the initial runway 'star', since the area inside the star had by then been fully developed.

Britain now has nineteen civil airports handling 300,000 or more passengers annually, with total traffic through all airports totalling ninety million passengers per year. Heathrow and Gatwick between them account for nearly two-thirds of the total.

BROADCASTING BUILDINGS

The history of public-service broadcasting in Britain dates from October 1922 with the licensing by Parliament of the BBC — the 'C' then stood for 'company' and it wasn't until 1927 that it became a public corporation. This was some thirty years after Marconi had first demonstrated wireless on the roof of the GPO's telegraphic headquarters in St Martin-le-Grand (see page 127, Post offices) and by that time, enthusiastic amateurs were busily using wireless sets to contact each other. Transmitters were springing up both in America and in Europe, including the Marconi Company's own station at Chelmsford which made its first broadcast in 1919, and the time was clearly ripe for the national service which the Post Office was instructed to supervise. The new company began life in offices on the second floor of Magnet House, the General Electrical Company's building in Kingsway in the Holborn district of London.

Its studios were round the corner on the top floor of Marconi House, on the corner of Aldwych and the Strand, from where the BBC broadcast its first programme, 'The News', on 14 November 1922. Marconi House was originally built in 1903 as the New Gaiety Hotel and Restaurant, on the site of the former Gaiety Theatre, with its elevations designed by R. Norman Shaw in a heavily Florentine/Renaissance style. The Marconi Company acquired and converted it in 1912, the prelude to a twenty-one-year occupancy. But within months the demands of efficiency made it essential to house both administrative and broadcasting functions in the same premises. In May 1923, therefore, the BBC moved to no 2 Savoy Hill, the west wing of the headquarters of the Institution of Electrical Engineers (IEE) in Savoy Place, which had acquired it in 1908 from the College of Physicians of London. The building had been put up in 1889 as the College's examination hall and education centre to the designs of Stephen Salter.

By 1926 there were five studios in operation at Savoy Hill which, it was becoming clear, would not be able to cope with the future growth of public service broadcasting. Accordingly the BBC began looking for a site in central London where a purpose-designed headquarters and studio complex could be built; it considered several existing buildings which proved too difficult to convert, and then in 1928 the site of Foley House became available for redevelopment, on the corner of Portland Place and Langham Street, south of Regent's Park — it was due, in fact, to be occupied by a block of luxury flats. The Corporation promptly acquired it for Broadcasting House, Britain's first dedicated broadcasting building. The design had to incorporate a modern look appropriate to the new science of broadcasting while harmonising with the Regency environment

14

of the surrounding buildings. The architect was Lt-Col G. Val Myer working in conjunction with the BBC's civil engineer, Marmaduke Tudsbery.

Internally the main challenge was to combine twenty-two broadcasting studios, which had to be completely acoustically insulated as well as air-conditioned, with administrative offices which needed to enjoy maximum natural daylighting. Myer's solution was to dispense with the inner lightwell which would normally have been necessary in a development of this scale, and to place the studios — for which artificial light was no disadvantage — in the core of the building. Here they were protected by an outer shell of offices which would act as an insulating shield. The studio core was planned as a separate brick building within this outer shell, with studio floors separated by libraries and stores for further acoustic isolation; the largest studio, the concert hall, occupied a volume of 3,540cu m (125,000cu ft) on three levels. Externally, the core is visible only on the Portland Place elevation where a short stretch of plain walling, inset with round windows, projects above the highest office storey. The air intakes of the ventilation system can be seen high up on the rear (Langham Street) elevation.

The building makes full use of its flatiron-shaped site with the main elevation, clad in Portland stone, following the curve of Portland Place to the blunted apex of the main entrance. Out of respect for the eighteenth-century origins of its neighbourhood, the windows are all individual, rather than arranged in the horizontal bands which might otherwise have been appropriate in a building of this period; and the southern rear elevation is stepped back to respect the rights

Plate 3 Broadcasting House from Regent Street. *(British Broadcasting Corporation)*

to light of nearby building owners. The overall effect has been aptly compared to one of the great white liners of the 1930s, sailing majestically towards the heart of London.

The carved panels at first floor level and over the main entrance are by the distinguished sculptor Eric Gill who adopted the BBC's suggestion that their subject should be Ariel, the invisible spirit of the air in Shakespeare's *The Tempest* and therefore an appropriate symbol for broadcasting. Broadcasting House went on the air with its first studio programme in 1932. Repaired after extensive war damage, it remains an important broadcasting centre.

Television was first demonstrated in 1926 by John Logie Baird, a Scottish engineer, at the Royal Institution in London. The first public demonstration by the BBC followed in 1929, and in 1935 the Government announced plans for a national service to be controlled by the BBC. After a period of experimental transmissions from various locations, including Savoy Hill and Broadcasting House, the BBC inaugurated the world's first regular TV service on 2 November 1936. The initial audience consisted of a few thousand viewers in the London area watching programmes made in studios at Alexandra Palace. The Palace first opened in 1873 as a Victorian entertainment centre — a north London equivalent of the Crystal Palace (see page 51, Exhibition centres). Originally designed by Alfred Meeson and J. Johnson it was constructed largely out of the buildings of the 1862 International Exhibition in Kensington and burned down almost immediately; redesigned by Johnson, it reopened two years later.

The Palace was never particularly successful, and its trustees were keen to alleviate their financial problems by letting out parts of the building for a commercial return. Standing on a hill 93m (306ft) above sea level, it was an ideal site for the BBC which needed height to ensure good reception for the ultra-high frequencies used in television. The Corporation leased an area of 5,110sq m (55,000sq ft) at the southern end of the Palace, including a large theatre, and rebuilt the south-east tower as five floors of offices, which also served as the base for a 91m (300ft) high steel aerial mast. This was the world's first television station. Alexandra Palace has retained its links with the BBC; until 1959 it was the headquarters of BBC TV News and the Corporation retains a transmitter on the site. The building suffered a second disastrous fire in 1980 and reconstruction began in 1984.

Television only became a national service after World War II, during which transmissions were suspended. The 1951 Festival of Britain helped popularise it, and by 1955 the Post Office had not only built a network of relay stations for the BBC covering virtually the whole of the UK, but was establishing a second network for the new independent companies being formed under the 1954 Television Act as a competing service, funded by advertising and not (as with the BBC) by licence payments from viewers. Its rôle has now passed to British Telecom.

The first independent companies went on the air in 1955, most of them broadcasting from existing buildings which were adapted. Associated Rediffusion in London called in the theatre architect Peter Moro to convert Adastral House,

Plate 4 The Granada site in Manchester; the first purpose-built TV complex in Europe (foreground) is now overshadowed by the later administration block. *(Granada Television Ltd)*

in Kingsway, an office building formerly occupied by the Air Ministry; while the cinema-operating company ABC used one of its own cinemas, the Capital at Didsbury, near Manchester, as the base for its weekend service in the north of England.

But one contractor had more ambitious ideas, and the first purpose-designed television building to become operational in Britain was the Manchester TV Centre, built by Granada to produce a weekday service in the north of England. The company put out its first programme from here on 3 May 1956, just under a year after securing its contract and seven months after Britain's first independent TV programme went out in London. The first phase of the new centre, the most modern TV complex in Europe at the time, took only seven months to build, on a 2ha (5 acre) piece of wasteland in Quay Street, Manchester — a few minutes' walk from the site of Britain's earliest railway station (see page 138, Railway stations). The architect was Ralph Tubbs, whose aim was that:

the TV Centre, as it grows, shall always retain a noble simplicity . . . The main buildings will thus be kept simple in outline and rely for their effect on the subtlety of their proportions and the texture of their walls.

The first building phase was a modest two-storey structure which, says Dennis Sharp in his book on Manchester, 'nevertheless created an impact in an area of dreary surroundings'. It was constructed on a frame of pre-cast concrete units fabricated off-site for speed of erection. The principal element was a double-height main studio 23.2 × 13.1 × 7.6m (76 × 43 × 25ft), the first custom-built TV studio in Britain and still in use. The Centre's Quay Street elevation was given full-height windows so that passers-by could glimpse something of the new world of television. The original building is now overshadowed by Granada's eight-storey administration block, completed in 1961; and in the course of developing its site into a 6ha (15 acre) broadcasting complex and tourist attraction, the company has taken over and converted many existing buildings, including an early iron-framed warehouse. The attractions include the British equivalent of a Hollywood back lot with reconstructions of the sets of popular TV programmes including the 'Rovers Return', the public house from Britain's longest-running soap opera *Coronation Street*, first shown in 1960; and a complete New York street scene screening a Victorian railway viaduct.

The Granada opening preceded that of the BBC's first purpose-designed television centre, even though this had been in the planning for seven years previously. In 1949 the BBC acquired a 5.4ha (13.5 acre) piece of land at Shepherd's Bush, on the site of the 1908 Franco-British Exhibition, for a replacement for Alexandra Palace. Progress was delayed, however, by government expenditure controls; work finally began in 1956 with the first studio programme going on the air from Shepherd's Bush in June 1960. The new complex, designed by Norman & Dawbarn, was built with studio blocks radiating outwards from a central administrative core to allow the easy movement of goods and heavy scenery around the perimeter.

Immediately north of the television centre is the BBC's White City development on the 6.5ha (16 acre) site of a former athletics ground and greyhound racing track. Designed by the BBC's own architects' department, with consultants Norman & Dawbarn and Scott Brownrigg & Turner, it contains a new corporate headquarters, a studio centre for TV news and current affairs, and a local radio network centre.

CINEMAS

The first demonstration of moving pictures in Britain took place in February 1896 at the Royal Polytechnic Institute (now the Regent Street Polytechnic) in central London. The following month came the first public showing at the Empire Music Hall, Leicester Square where films became regular features of the nightly variety programmes during the course of the year. The Empire had opened twelve years earlier; designed by the theatre architect Thomas Verity, it occupied the shell of the circular Royal London Panorama built in 1881 for the public display of panoramic paintings, an earlier form of visual entertainment which was already nearing the end of its popularity. By 1925 thousands of purpose-built cinemas had opened throughout the UK, and the Empire had finally realised the destiny implicit in its early flirtation with film — it was acquired by the American MGM Film Corporation who closed it in 1927 and redeveloped the site as a cinema which could seat audiences of up to 3,500.

The rebuilding was handled by the Scots-born Thomas W. Lamb, who became the first and most prominent cinema architect in America. Working under the auspices of Frank Matcham, Britain's greatest theatre designer who had died in 1920, he produced a building which, with its Renaissance façade and lavish interior could justifiably bill itself as the 'Showplace of the Nation'; it was later remodelled by Verity's son Frank. The Empire's reign lasted from 1928 until 1961 when, with cinema attendances throughout Britain declining in the face of competition from television, it was again remodelled by George Coles. The interior was gutted to create two separate and independent places of entertainment. The upper levels of the former theatre became a new cinema auditorium, capable of seating 1,330 and with its own licensed bar, which reopened in 1962. Below, the stalls were converted into a ballroom. The history of the Empire is typical of the early advance of the cinema, rivalling and often taking over its predecessors, the theatre and the music hall, and drawing from them its architecture of ornate façades and opulent interiors.

In the early days, however, public demand for the new entertainment was so great that almost any venue would do. Enterprising showmen were quick to see the potential: they converted shops which became known as 'penny gaffs' because of their customary admission charge, and roller skating rinks (these had first come into fashion in the 1870s — The Dome at Worthing, Sussex was converted in 1921); hired town halls or vacant buildings; projected against walls in the open air; and toured with travelling filmshows. Considerable effort and expense went into attracting customers. The 'penny gaffs' were often enhanced with ornate fronts and elevated titles — such as 'The Electric Palace' — while the touring shows were staged, typically, in elaborate structures, seating audiences of up to 1,000 and drawing large crowds every night by their effective use of external illumination. They created a mass audience for a new generation of permanent buildings; however, concern for public safety brought regulation in the form of the 1909 Cinematograph Act which specified the number of exits from the auditorium and, more important, required the separation and fireproofing of the projection booth — (early films were produced on highly inflammable stock.)

The earliest purpose-built cinemas on record predated the 1909 Act. David Atwell, an authority on the subject, has tracked down two in Portsmouth, Hampshire which opened in 1901 and gave regular nightly programmes: the Portland Hall (800 seats) which closed in 1920; and The Victoria, which did not survive the 1950s. No description has survived the years of either, but many of the early purpose-built cinemas were basic brick or corrugated iron sheds behind façades which ranged from the functional to the elaborate. The oldest extant purpose-built cinema building in Britain is The Electric in Portobello Road, north Kensington, which opened in 1905; although extensively rebuilt in 1910 the shell may well be original. The Electric is a simple, hall-like building with a vaulted ceiling, ornamented with plasterwork. It is listed for preservation because of its architectural and historic interest, but it closed as a cinema in 1987.

The oldest surviving purpose-built cinema which is substantially unaltered

Plate 5 The front of the Electric Palace Cinema, Harwich, the oldest, largely unaltered cinema building still showing films. (*Chris Strachan*)

and which, more important, is still fulfilling its original function is the Electric Palace in Harwich, Essex. Built in 1911 in a side street of the East Anglian port at a cost of £1,500 it was the first major building designed by Harold Ridley Hooper; basically nothing more than a brick shed, it rises above its side-street location boasting an ornate front with piers and garlands in locally quarried Roman cement under a semicircular pediment. David Atwell describes it as 'the epitome of the pre-First World War cinema'. It was closed in 1956, but was rediscovered in 1972 in the course of an architectural survey of Harwich, rescued from plans for a car park, statutorily listed as a building of sociological interest, and reopened in 1981 after restoration.

Purpose-built auditoria were comparatively rare in the early days of the cinema, partly because of the plentiful supply of existing buildings which could be converted. The most historic building to have served as a cinema is St Nicholas' Chapel in Chester, which dates back to the thirteenth century. Used after the Reformation as the city's Common Hall (town hall), it became a theatre in the eighteenth century; after substantial rebuilding in 1854–5, it reopened as a music room. Following a spell as a temporary Catholic church, it was finally used as a cinema between 1915 and 1961; it is now a shop.

The oldest building still showing films is the Picture Playhouse in Beverley, Humberside; it was built originally in 1886 as the town's Corn Exchange, opened as a cinema in 1911 and reopened in 1982 after serving as a bingo hall, having been reprieved from redevelopment. The first theatre to be adapted permanently as a cinema was the 'Theatre Royal' in the Attercliffe district of Sheffield, south Yorkshire; designed by Flockton Gibbs and Flockton and originally opened in 1897, it was shortly after that remodelled by Frank Matcham and reopened in 1907; it was destroyed by fire in 1935. Theatres and music halls were obvious candidates for conversion, and continued to be adapted into the early 1930s alongside the development of increasingly ambitious purpose-built cinemas which were modelled on theatres.

Between the two world wars, the industry expanded dramatically to accommodate public demand for what it was to become — the first of the modern mass media. By the time that the Empire, Leicester Square was reborn in 1925 cinemas were established as a distinct building type, expressed in architectural styles including the classical, Moorish, Renaissance and picturesque. In 1928 the 'talkies' set the scene for a new generation of super-cinemas, the model for which was the Regent at Brighton, completed seven years earlier to the design of Robert Atkinson. In size, architectural treatment and prominent location, the super-cinema was expressly designed to attract mass attendances, and they provided the chief source of public entertainment for the next half century. Their audiences were numbered in thousands, and would progress through impressive foyers to auditoria which resembled theatres in their fan-shaped plans and proscenium arches (introduced to house sound equipment). They were designed in styles ranging from Renaissance to underwater fantasy; some had restaurants or cafés; but from the outset, all were planned to create a sense of occasion.

At the outbreak of World War II there were some 5,500 cinemas in Britain;

Plate 6 The Point at Milton Keynes, Buckinghamshire, with the building containing Britain's first purpose-designed multiscreen cinema to the left. *(Higgs and Hill plc)*

the total is now around 1,000. By the end of the 1950s the great age was over, its close signalled by the twin advances of television as the new medium of mass entertainment, and of bingo as the sole salvation of hundreds of buildings that would otherwise have been lost — the first (Rank) bingo hall opened in Peckham in 1961 in a converted cinema. The New Victoria, close to London's Victoria Station and completed in 1930 to the design of E. Walmsley Lewis, has survived by putting history into reverse and becoming a theatre. One of the few cinemas statutorily listed for preservation as a dramatic example of the international modern style, it closed in 1976 but, after a short-lived experiment with pop concerts, reopened to stage theatrical spectaculars.

Outside the West End of London, the super-cinemas that have survived as film theatres have done so by being subdivided into smaller auditoria offering alternative programmes. New purpose-designed cinemas are invariably multiscreen, a form pioneered in the USA, and are often an integral part of a whole entertainment complex with restaurants, nightclubs and bars. Both developments are evidence of the revival the industry began to experience in the late 1960s, which came about as the major cinema-owning chains realised that greater choice was essential to attract customers in an age of multi-channel television. The first purpose-designed multiplex cinema, with ten screens, opened

22

in 1985 at The Point, a modern entertainment complex in the new city of Milton Keynes, Buckinghamshire.

The Point claims to be the first purpose-planned integrated leisure centre in Europe, and was developed at a cost of £9 million by the brewing group subsidiary Bass Leisure and American Multi-Cinema — this company originated the first multi-screen movie theatre in the USA in Kansas City, Missouri, in 1963. The Point consists of two buildings linked by a mall: in front, rising 21.3m (70ft) high under a lattice-steel frame shaped like a pyramid and — as a visual draw — painted bright red, is a stepped ziggurat with three tiers of entertainment suites: a nightclub at the apex, situated above restaurants and bars at middle level, with a 1,500-seater bingo hall at the lowest level. At the rear, and entered via the connecting mall, is a rectangular box containing the ten cinema auditoria with total seating accommodation of over 2,000. The Point was designed by Birmingham interior designer Neil Tibbatts, working in conjunction with architects Building Design Partnership.

CIVIC BUILDINGS

The oldest civic building in Britain with a continuous history is the Guildhall of the City of London, the City being the first municipality to achieve the right to local self-government. It was built between 1411 and 1440 to the designs of John Croxton, close to the site of a building dating back at least to 1128 in which Henry FitzAilwyn, the first Mayor (the title Lord Mayor does not appear until 1283), was installed in 1191. The earlier Guildhall was described by a contemporary chronicler, Robert Fabyan, as 'an old and little cottage', as compared to Croxton's design which was 'a fair and goodly house'.

Judging from its name, it had presumably once belonged to one of the City guilds or confraternities of merchants and craftsmen which, in the form of livery companies (so called after the distinctive livery or uniform once worn by their members), continue to play an important part in the ceremonial life of the City. Some of these guilds may have originated in Saxon times, and there is evidence that the City first began to enjoy a degree of self-government during the reign of Alfred the Great. By the time of the Norman Conquest, the City of London was a power in the land, and William the Conqueror chose to avoid direct conflict with its citizens by granting them a royal charter and guaranteeing their rights and privileges; significantly, too, he built the Tower of London (see page 61, Fortresses) outside their boundaries.

Completed in 1440, the hall was a proud and confident statement of the power and wealth of the medieval City of London. Stone built (in itself a rarity for a secular building of the time), at over 46m (152ft) it was over half the length of Westminster Hall with which it was clearly intended to invite comparison, and served the same function — a place for meetings and ceremonies. Lit by two rows of windows (some glazed with glass, then an expensive commodity) it was paved with good-quality Purbeck stone — further evidence that cost was no object to the City authorities of the day who were able to finance the construction work through gifts, bequests and special levies. Part of the vaulted undercroft survives, as does the fifteenth-century porch with its largely original interior which is still the main entrance from Guildhall Yard — but the hall itself was badly damaged in the Great Fire of 1666. The main external walls, however, survived and in the reconstruction, which was probably supervised (if not designed) by Wren, these were raised by 6m (20ft) to allow room for a new tier, a line of round-arched Roman windows above the level of the medieval cornice. At the same time a new flat roof was built.

Over the next two centuries the Guildhall enjoyed periodic embellishment: in 1788–9 it acquired an elaborate new front designed by George Dance the

Younger, whose father was the architect of the nearby Mansion House, the Lord Mayor's official residence; and in 1862 the City's architect Sir Horace Jones replaced the post-Fire flat roof with an open one — historically more apt — in the style of Westminster Hall; he also introduced a minstrels' gallery. Damage sustained from World War II bombing was repaired under the direction of Sir Giles Gilbert Scott whose report on the condition of the building recorded the 'remarkable fact' that 'the medieval portions of the old Hall remain intact and practically uninjured'. The Guildhall survives today as an historic jewel, set in a precinct of later buildings of varying architectural quality which today provide offices for the administration of the City of London, and also the Guildhall library (see page 83, Libraries).

Elsewhere in Britain, from the twelfth century onwards, towns such as Chester and York were following the example of London and achieving local self-government, although their civic buildings generally remained modest structures. There were, however, exceptions such as the Guildhall in York, completed nine years after the City of London's which it approached in size and dignity. The medieval type of town hall had a single meeting room above a ground floor which might be used as a prison or to store market stalls, and this sufficed most communities, particularly as towns outside London did not attain the size or economic importance of their European counterparts until they began to benefit from the prosperity and population movements generated by the Industrial Revolution, and the institution of municipal democracy which

Plate 7 The fifteenth-century Gothic porch of the City of London Guildhall. *(City of London Corporation)*

followed. Anyway, it was not until 1851 that a census first showed more than fifty per cent of Britons to be living in towns as opposed to the countryside.

Among the earliest municipal buildings reflecting the dawning of a new civic awareness were the first Liverpool town hall designed by John Wood the elder, and the Berwick-upon-Tweed town hall, both completed in 1754. But pre-nineteenth-century local government was a long way from the wide-ranging social engine which it later became, with responsibilities for public health and education, welfare, housing and town planning. When the Birmingham town hall was completed in 1835, a single basement committee room was sufficient for the management of the public and social needs of a population of just under 150,000. The building was designed in the form of a Roman temple by Hansom & Welch, and maintained the practice of dual use by having the upper part as a concert hall, thus continuing the eighteenth-century tradition of having assembly halls, acquired or built by town corporations as amenities for their growing populations. The most splendid realisation of dual-purpose civic architecture is St George's Hall in Liverpool, conceived shortly after Birmingham's town hall and completed in 1856. It was designed in Grecian style by Harvey Lonsdale Elmes who was in his early twenties when he won the competition; it combined a concert hall and law courts in one.

The completion of the Birmingham town hall (which was almost immediately extended) coincided with the Municipal Reform Act which came into force in 1835 — one of the great battery of reforms in the nineteenth century which established local government as we know it today by creating newly constituted municipal corporations governed by elected councils. Initially these coexisted with the so-called Boards of Commissioners already providing recognised local government functions — street paving and improvements, for example — but they steadily acquired sole responsibility for a widening range of functions, which eventually could no longer be organised from a single meeting room but needed separate administrative offices and staff. The earliest town hall to recognise and adapt to this practical need as well as continuing to embody the formal, ceremonial rôle of a civic building was Leeds. Completed in 1858 it was designed by Cuthbert Brodrick who in 1852 had won the first-ever architectural competition staged for a municipal building of this scale. Sir Charles Barry assessed the competition and later summed up the rôle of the town hall as he and the Victorian age in general saw it:

> A town hall should in my opinion be the most dominant and important of the municipal buildings of the city in which it is placed. It should be the means of giving due expression to public feeling upon all national and municipal events of importance . . . [It should serve] as it were as the exponent of the life and soul of the city.

Leeds is a classical monument to civic pride and purpose. In the words of the chairman of the committee appointed to oversee the project: 'We are about to erect this town hall, first as an ornamental building, and in order that the . . . business of the borough may be concentrated in one building, and thereby

Plate 8 Leeds Town Hall, the earliest in Britain designed with offices for local government administration. *(Leeds City Council)*

be done better and cheaper than it could be were it otherwise.' Built largely in local Yorkshire stone, the dominant external feature is a tower 68.5m (225ft) high which was added to the original design at the suggestion of Barry and rapidly established itself as an essential landmark in the spate of Victorian town halls which followed the example of Leeds. Its importance as a symbol of nascent municipal confidence was attested by the fact that Queen Victoria and Prince Albert came to perform the opening ceremony.

Internally, a central assembly room was ringed by offices and committee rooms. There was a council chamber, mayoral suite, and courts. All the necessary facilities for civic celebration and administration were therefore present, although the offices were limited in number and not allocated to specific departments (town clerk, borough treasurer and borough surveyor) until after their completion. The building can therefore be seen as transitional in so far as it foreshadowed the future administrative town hall, as well as being 'the last of a more formal type containing little in the way of offices' — in the words of Dr Colin Cunningham who has researched the subject.

The need for office accommodation grew in parallel with a stream of municipal legislation typified by the 1848 Health Act which imposed new responsibilities on local authorities and created corresponding public services. In Leeds itself, a second competition was staged in 1876 for an additional block of public offices; these were completed in 1884, and followed in turn by a third block. In the end, the Leeds municipal complex occupied an entire island site in the heart of the city. Later, town halls such as Manchester's (completed 1877; architect Alfred Waterhouse) were built from the outset on a much grander scale to provide more office accommodation; while the need to take advantage of sometimes awkwardly shaped sites and to plan internal spaces more flexibly led in turn to a preference for the Gothic style, as opposed to the more formal classicism of the Leeds hall and its predecessors.

By the early twentieth century, local authorities were recognising the impossibility of housing administrative, legal and cultural functions within a single structure. The solution was the civic centre, a planned grouping of separate but related buildings such as had already occurred informally in the extensions and additions made to the town halls in Birmingham and Leeds. The first to be conceived and planned on the grand scale was at Cardiff, the capital of Wales.

In 1898 the city council acquired the 24ha (59 acre) Cathays Park estate in the centre of Cardiff from the Marquess of Bute, whose family had owned it since 1793. The following year the city engineer produced plans for laying out the land: along the southern boundary close to Cardiff Castle would be the first great trio of buildings — the Renaissance-style city hall (1906; by Lanchester, Stewart & Rickards), flanked by the law courts (designed contemporaneously by the same architects), and the National Museum of Wales (architects A. D. Smith and C. Brewer; opened in 1927 after delays caused by World War I). Behind these, on either side of a central public garden, are a cluster of mostly university buildings dating from 1903; finally the northern range is devoted to government offices, the most recent block of which was completed in 1980 — an eighty-year record of progressive civic development.

DEPARTMENT STORES

Department stores emerged during the nineteenth century as a result of the enterprise and ambition of small shopkeepers, most of whom were drapers — although Harrods began life in 1849 as a grocer's. As these prospered they added new lines and, by acquiring adjoining properties, gradually spread along shopping streets. Their customers were the newly affluent middle classes, both city dwellers and shoppers from the suburbs and country who, with the spread of the railways from the 1830s onwards, could come up for the day by train and travel on to the shops by horse-drawn omnibus. The stores used their buying power to offer plenty of choice and quality at low cost and they duly prospered.

Among the enterprising drapers, many of whom first set up in business in the previous century, were some who were to become famous names. In 1778 the forerunner of Debenhams opened up in Wigmore Street, north of London's Oxford Street, while in 1790 Dickins & Smith (later Dickins & Jones) started in business with a single shop in Oxford Street; in 1835 they moved to Regent Street. The oldest firm to begin trading on the lines of a modern department store was the predecessor of Kendals, still the leading store in Manchester. In 1796 John Watts, a yeoman farmer of Didsbury (then a village to the south of Manchester), moved up to the city and opened a drapery shop in Deansgate. He prospered and soon moved to larger rented premises on the opposite side of the same street — no 99, called Brook's Bazaar, where his sons Samuel and James joined him in the business.

In 1831 the Watts redeveloped their premises as a purpose-designed, three-storeyed building which they continued to call 'The Bazaar' and where they advertised themselves as selling 'the most fashionable article in every branch of art of manufacture, at a reasonable rate'. The Bazaar operated on the 'shops within shops' concession principle common to modern department stores, with individual traders renting counters to sell their goods under the Watts' overall management. Among the managers they brought in to help the enterprise were three young men called Thomas Kendal, James Milne and Alan Faulkner who joined in 1830. The trio were good at their jobs and towards the end of 1835 bought the business from their employers, reopening it the following January with the first-ever New Year Sale in Britain.

The Kendal, Milne & Faulkner Bazaar flourished and the new owners soon took advantage of the opportunity to acquire the shop next door. In 1872 the original buildings were demolished and replaced by a new store designed by E. J. Thomson which the firm's local newspaper advertising announced as 'a stately four-storey building with elegantly appointed windows, where ladies of fashion alight from their carriages'. This, too, expanded along the street and was finally replaced in 1940, by which time Kendals (which was acquired by Harrods soon after World War I) had long since occupied premises on both sides of Deansgate.

In 1877, five years after Kendals was redeveloped following its initial expansion, Britain acquired its first department store to be planned and built as such from the outset. This was Bon Marché, built in the centre of Brixton, south London, by James 'Rosebery' Smith, a local printer and publisher who financed it from his racecourse winnings at Newmarket. Bon Marché was consciously modelled by its architects Parsons and Rawlings along the lines of the flourishing Parisian store of the same name. This French venture had been opened in 1852 as a piece-goods store by an energetic husband-and-wife team, the Boucicauts; it had expanded rapidly into additional lines and departments, and in 1876 had moved into new premises in the Rue de Sèvres.

In *The Golden Age of Shop Design* Alexandra Artley gives the Boucicauts credit for pioneering . . .

> . . . the idea of the department store as a building purposely designed for fashionable public assembly and which, by the use of display techniques and eye-catching design which developed rapidly over the next decades, supplanted the commercial principle of supply with that of consumer seduction.

Britain's equivalent began under equally optimistic auguries. It was described in *The Builder* on 24 March 1877 as a

> large and handsome new market building . . . a novelty in market accommodation in the metropolis, embracing the sale of almost every imaginable article . . . under one management. Both the main frontages — the one facing Brixton Road and the other Shepherd's Lane — have some architectural pretensions, the latter being the most prominent of the two, in consequence of being surmounted by lofty mansard roofs.

The store cost £70,000 to build and occupied an area of former nursery gardens bounded by the main railway line into London Victoria — which was why, with a station at Brixton, this formerly rural suburb developed so rapidly in the latter part of the nineteenth century. With its brick elevations enhanced by granite pilasters, columns, window dressings of Portland stone and shell-based balconies, Bon Marché was designed to impress the growing local population and persuade them that it was not necessary to cross the river into the West End to find the choice and quality of shopping which they required.

The Builder goes into useful detail on the store's internal arrangements. The front part of the basement and the north side of the ground floor were divided up into small specialist departments, while the rest of the ground storey and the upper floors were open plan in the manner of modern stores. At the rear were bedrooms and dining rooms for living-in staff. Bon Marché also enjoyed sophisticated fire precautions with a 27,275 litre (6,000 gallon) water tank installed under the roof to feed a sprinkler system 'communicating with every part of the

Plate 9 Bon Marché, Brixton, the earliest purpose-designed department store. *(Watts and Partners)*

building'. In spite of its novelty and the care that went into the design, Bon Marché was soon eclipsed by the West End stores which were engaged in major rebuildings, and turned out to be a financial disaster for 'Rosebery' Smith who went bankrupt in 1892.

The store was then acquired by a consortium of retailers, passing in time into the ownership of the John Lewis Group which finally closed it in 1975. But this was not the end of the story, for in October 1984 the building became the home of the Brixton Enterprise Centre, a joint employment-creation venture between BAT Industries Small Businesses Ltd and Lambeth Borough Council. The two sponsors spent £3 million on restoring and modernising the building, with chartered building surveyors Watts and Partners as designers and supervisors of the conversion. It is now the home of 150 small businesses which provide employment for over 300 local people. On the ground floor at the Brixton Road frontage are shops which operate in the form of a managed market, with studios, offices and craft workshops above and at the rear. In its present form, therefore, Bon Marché operates in its retail areas along the same principles as those established at the opening of the original Manchester Bazaar.

Because of its location (Brixton was ceasing to be a fashionable area by the early twentieth century) and the physical restrictions on its site, Bon Marché could never have developed into a major department store of the kind that within a generation of its opening, were dominating the shopping centres of the major towns and cities. In London, the new Harrods opened in 1905; it was followed four years later by Selfridges — founded by the American store magnate Gordon Selfridge, this was the first in the West End to open in its own buildings and the largest department store ever built in Britain as a single entity (though the original front was less than half the length of the present Oxford Street elevation). Selfridges adopted a novel approach to customers, who were encouraged to browse (instead of being pressured to buy the moment they set foot inside, as in rival stores) and were offered the comforts of four lounges, a library and an information bureau; Selfridge, who enjoyed expressing himself in pithy sayings, summed it all up with the comment 'this is not a shop — it's a community centre'.

Selfridges was designed by a trio of architects from both sides of the Atlantic: Daniel H. Burnham, the design chief of the 1893 World Columbian Exposition in Chicago; a young Canadian Francis S. Swales; and R. Frank Atkinson, the British architect of the Waring-White contracting company which built the store. Swales' contribution, inspired by his time as a student in Paris, was the grand procession of Ionic columns running along the main elevations and rising through three storeys from first-floor level; these made the store so instantly recognisable as to obviate the need for displaying its name on the fascia (to which Selfridge was opposed). The innovatory steel frame was designed by the Swedish-American consulting engineer Sven Bylander. Selfridges was extended to its present size during the period between the two world wars.

DOCKS

The earliest ports of any maritime nation developed in the open waters of natural harbours or the tidal estuaries of navigable rivers. Plymouth had an international port as early as 900–800BC at Mount Batten, at the mouth of the River Plym; the River Thames was the decisive factor in the development of London; and the estuary of the Mersey the key to the growth of Liverpool. The Romans founded London around AD50, because it particularly had two great advantages: first, the river at that point ran deep and wide enough to accommodate large vessels from the great trading rivers of western Europe — the Rhine and the Schelde — which lay opposite its mouth. And second, London was the first point upstream where the Thames could be conveniently bridged — in the early years of their occupation, the Romans built the first London Bridge (of timber) close to where its modern successor now stands.

London therefore flourished both as a natural port and as the ideal centre for a national road network, and as early as AD61 it was 'frequented by many merchants and trading vessels', according to the Roman historian Tacitus. As in other great estuarine ports, seaborne trade was initially handled in one of two ways: either ships remained in mid-stream and were loaded and offloaded by lighters (small cargo boats); or they moored at wharves built in timber or stone on the river banks, timing their arrivals and departures by the tides. The earliest dock structures, therefore, consisted of these wharves and the warehouses built alongside them to store goods after they were landed, or prior to their transhipment.

Archaeological investigation has shown that Roman quays ran along the north bank of the Thames upstream from the present-day site of the Tower, and excavations have unearthed quay walls built of squared oak beams arranged in tiers. London was also the leading port of the Saxons and the Venerable Bede, writing in the eighth century in his *Ecclesiastical History of England*, described it as 'a market of many nations, coming by land and sea'. Remains of the Anglo-Saxon port, in the form of timbers which formed a seventh-century quay, have been discovered below the Strand, upstream of the Roman ones.

The Normans inherited a bustling international port, but its future expansion was determined by the design and building of the first stone London Bridge between 1176 and 1209. Its large, narrow arches were a deterrent to navigation and ensured that, from then on, large vessels would have to berth below the bridge at wharves such as Billingsgate — a commercial centre by the year AD1000 — while up-river traffic had to use Queenhithe, above the bridge, which had been handling commercial shipping in the reign of King Alfred. In

London and other port cities, riverside wharves remained in use until well into the nineteenth century, although by then the vast bulk of maritime commerce was being handled in the enclosed dock systems; these, along with the canals, were the greatest civil engineering achievements of the pre-railway era. The excavation of docks, with lock gates enabling them to be closed off from open water, was to make shipping independent of the tides for the first time.

The earliest example, however, was planned for shipbuilding rather than cargo handling: the first commercial enclosed dock in Britain was built in about 1660 by the East India Company (see page 103, Offices) at Blackwall, on the north bank of the River Thames 5km (3 miles) east of London Bridge. The constructional principles were in fact familiar because of the enclosed dock built earlier in the century at the nearby Royal Naval Shipyard at Deptford, on the south bank. Blackwall Dock was small, with a basin only 0.6ha (1.5 acres) in area and no cargo quays, since it was intended solely for the fitting out and repair of company ships. However, in 1789 a private speculator, John Perry, enlarged it to an area of 3.25ha (8 acres) to service the company's expanding fleet, which included the largest ships then using the Thames. The resulting Brunswick Dock (named after one of the German duchies of the Hanoverian dynasty) later became the nucleus of the East India Docks which opened in 1806 — four years after the West Indias which were London's first enclosed docks designed for commercial traffic.

But London was nearly one hundred years behind Liverpool, where work began in 1710 on what had become a complete dock system by the end of the century — the first in Britain to be built as such. Liverpool, too insignificant for mention in the Domesday Book and an agricultural community throughout the Middle Ages, had become a substantial town by the seventeenth century. The main reason for this growth, as with London, was its river — the Mersey — which offered a viable alternative when Chester, the main historic port of north-west England, became unusable because of the progressive silting up of the River Dee.

Another boost to the town's fortunes resulted from the series of disasters suffered by London — the plague of 1665 and the Great Fire of 1666 — which provoked merchants into finding an alternative base for trading with the New World. They no doubt gave their new colleagues vivid descriptions of the congestion and delays which were endemic in the port of London — these were due to the virtual monopoly enjoyed by the 'legal quays' which prevented proper docks being built, and forced large ships to moor in midstream and be laboriously and vulnerably loaded and unloaded by traditional methods.

By the end of the century Liverpool had eclipsed Chester and was an international customs port in its own right, but with a pressing need to provide better accommodation for a growing maritime traffic and thus avoid incurring London's problems. Its solution was to build an enclosed trading dock within the area of the Pool, a creek of the Mersey which was the historic harbour of Liverpool. The contract was given to Thomas Steers, the city's first dock engineer, with George Sorocold, the leading hydraulic engineer of the period, as adviser;

work began in 1710. Construction was difficult since the dock was being built actually in a waterway, and it did not open until 1715 (and then at first only partially). Roughly rectangular, the Old Dock had a water area of 1.5ha (3.5 acres) enclosed behind brick walls and was entered through a tidal basin. A plan of 1725 shows that it was capable of accommodating fourteen merchant sailing vessels.

By the early nineteenth century the Old Dock had been outgrown by the continuing expansion of the port. In 1826 it was finally filled in — the site is now occupied by Canning Place — but it continued to influence the construction of the rest of the Liverpool docks since the level of its sill was used as the datum throughout the system for the next hundred years. Development of Liverpool's South Docks, as they became known, continued into the early twentieth century, by which time the port was second only to London. The South Docks eventually stretched for 5.5km (3.5 miles) along the eastern bank of the Mersey, the land on which they were built having been reclaimed.

The later North Docks extended for a similar distance in the opposite direction, the most recent and northerly being the Royal Seaforth Dock opened in 1972; a 34ha (85 acre) basin equipped with modern cargo handling, container and roll-on/roll-off (ro-ro) terminals. The original South Docks finally closed to commercial traffic in 1972 after a long decline; built for sailing ships, they were too small and shallow for modern purposes and the bulk of the port's trade had long since shifted to the larger, more recent northern docks system. In 1981 they were handed over to the Merseyside Development Corporation which had been established to oversee the regeneration of the redundant docklands.

London's docklands have had a shorter history, despite the rapid initial pace of development — Parliament had responded in 1799 to the growing competition from Liverpool and other ports (notably Bristol) and had finally allowed the construction of commercial docks in the capital. The opening in 1802 of the West Indias was followed in quick succession by the London Docks (1805), the East India Docks (1806), Surrey Docks (1807, on the south bank of the Thames), St Katharine Dock (1828), Victoria Dock (1855), Millwall Docks (1868), and Albert Dock (1880). The St Katharine Dock, excavated on the site of a royal hospital founded in 1148, represented a new departure — it was built complete with substantial warehouses which were ranged along the quayside for the easier handling of cargo, hoisted directly from hold to storage. The dock basin was designed by the engineer Thomas Telford and the buildings by Thomas Aitchison and Philip Hardwick. Only the magnificent Ivory House now remains of these (St Katharine was badly bombed in World War II after being in decline for some years previously) but the idea of building docks and warehouses as a single entity was taken up at Liverpool where the Albert Dock is preserved in its entirety (see below).

The final stage in the development of the Port of London came in 1886 when new docks were built 42km (26 miles) down-river at Tilbury, which was eventually to supersede the upstream basins. In the 1960s the Port of London spent £30 million on improving Tilbury so that it could handle the new generation of

Plate 10 Liverpool's Albert Dock, the earliest surviving collection of integral dock warehouses in Britain's first planned commercial dock system, reborn in the 1980s as a shopping and leisure complex which houses the Merseyside Maritime Museum and the Tate Gallery of the North. *(Tate Gallery, Liverpool)*

Plate 11 The Italianate Ivory House at St Katharine Dock, London, a survivor of the earliest integral dock/warehouse grouping in Britain, now converted into shops, offices, luxury apartments and a yacht club. *(St Katharine-by-the Tower Ltd)*

container ships, which could then be turned around in thirty-six hours rather than days, as was previously the case. Within two decades, the inland docks which had brought prosperity to London and Britain's other great port cities had gone, ousted by modern complexes such as Tilbury and (in Liverpool) Seaforth which were conveniently located at coastal or near-coastal sites for the bulk movement of goods carried by modern container and ro-ro ships, with fast inland road and rail connections throughout the country. London's inland docks all closed between 1967 and 1982, as did the South Docks in Liverpool.

Their obsolescence has, however, created a rare planning opportunity and the historic city docklands have fostered some of the most ambitious exercises in urban renewal in Britain. The largest of these is in London, where the London Docklands Development Corporation was formed in 1981 to oversee the regeneration of 20sq km (8sq miles) of redundant industrial land into a new business city. St Katharine Dock was the pioneering example in Britain of dockland regeneration, and had already shown what could be done: after its closure in 1968, the former Greater London Council had acquired the 10ha (25 acre) site and had staged a competition for its redevelopment; this was won by Taylor Woodrow. Beginning in 1970, this company and its architects, the Renton, Howard, Wood, Levin Partnership, converted the Ivory House (dating from 1854) into shops, offices and apartments; built new office and residential blocks and tourist attractions along the other quays; and turned the dock basin into the first yacht marina in central London.

In Liverpool, the 1984 Liverpool Garden Festival took place on former dockland and the Festival Park remains as a permanent improvement. The Albert Dock, opened in 1846 and originally designed by Jesse Hartley and Philip Chadwick, was the first in Liverpool to be built complete with warehouses — these now constitute the largest concentration of Grade I-listed buildings in Britain. The Arrowcroft Group, working in partnership with the Merseyside Development Corporation and with the Franklin Stafford Partnership as their architects, has transformed Albert Dock into a thriving shopping, business and entertainment centre; it is situated only a few minutes from the heart of Liverpool but without the loss of any of the buildings, some of which make fitting homes for such institutions as the Merseyside Maritime Museum and the Tate Gallery of the North.

Urban renewal of the redundant inland docklands is an attractive proposition precisely because industrial usage kept them comparatively undeveloped during the modern commercial expansion of the cities. With large areas of potentially valuable land lying close to city centres in appealing waterside locations, they offer opportunities to plan new business and residential communities without the disruption caused by wholesale redevelopment, and to exploit the economic re-use of some of the most dramatic monuments of Britain's industrial heritage.

EDUCATION BUILDINGS

Buildings designed specifically for the education of children did not emerge as a distinct building type until after the fourteenth century. Before then, to quote Malcolm Seaborne in *The English School*, 'very little provision was needed by way of equipment or buildings'. Teaching was largely oral until copybooks for exercises and printed text books became generally available during the fifteenth century, and the only furnishings and equipment considered necessary were benches for the pupils (almost exclusively boys), the master's chair and his bundle of birch rods — the last considered so essential, and used so regularly, as an educational tool that it appears proudly flourished in contemporary illustrations of schools and even on their official seals. One room, often inside another building such as a church or cathedral, was usually all that was necessary for the small numbers of children being educated outside their homes.

The King's School at Canterbury was founded in AD598 as an annexe of the cathedral. Almost contemporary with the re-establishment of Christianity, its original objective was the training of future churchmen. The school was reorganised after the Norman Conquest by Archbishop Lanfranc, who provided space for it in his new archiepiscopal palace. Refounded in 1541 during the dissolution of the monasteries, the school now occupies the precincts of the cathedral and the palace with the Mint Yard as its centre. All early schools were religious foundations, among them the choir schools which supplied the need for trained choristers to sing the sacred office and liturgy of the Mass.

The earliest school to be planned and built as an educational institution is Winchester College, Hampshire, established in 1382 by William of Wykeham, Bishop of Winchester and twice Lord Chancellor, who was also the founder of the related New College at Oxford (see page 41, Universities), the two forming a continuous educational sequence. Like New College, Winchester was in its origins a religious community, only some of whose members were concerned with the education of the ninety-six boys. The teaching staff were members of the community and lived in the college, where the seventy scholars boarded. The original schoolroom, 'the only ancient school building of the fourteenth century now existing' according to J. H. Leach, was completed in 1394. It lay below the hall in which the scholars ate with the rest of the community, and was a single room 13.8 by 8.8 by 4.6m (45½ by 29 by 15ft), lit by three windows in the south wall. Below these windows, tiers of stone benches allowed prefects the advantage of height in overseeing their less senior fellow pupils.

In this simple room the boys were taught all together by the master and his assistant, their course of study being concerned mainly with Latin grammar.

They slept in six dormitories on the ground floor of a range of buildings across the main college courtyard (Chamber Court), and joined the rest of the community in the chapel next to their schoolroom for religious services. (Eton College, founded in 1440, followed a similar pattern.) The original schoolroom was reduced in length in 1687 when a new passage was constructed, connecting the Chamber Court with a new, larger schoolroom completed that year in a detached building to the south of the court, and designed to accommodate several classes working together; the architect was possibly Wren. Its predecessor was then used as an additional dormitory, and from 1701 it was known as 'the seventh chamber'; it is now used for studies.

The oldest distinct school building still in educational use is the Pedagogue's House at the King Edward VI School in Stratford-upon-Avon, Warwickshire; it was founded in 1296 by the Guild of the Holy Cross, a charitable religious fraternity, and served by a community or 'college' of priests. The school originally used existing community buildings, but in 1427 the Guild completed a two-storeyed schoolhouse in half-timbered construction. In 1553, teaching moved into the fifteenth-century Guildhall (where Shakespeare was taught) and the schoolhouse

Plate 12 The Chamber Court of Winchester College, looking towards the chapel, hall and entrance to the original schoolroom. *(Winchester College)*

became the home of the schoolmaster or 'pedagogue'. It came back into school use in the nineteenth century and is now used as administrative offices.

The Tudor period was one of significant developments in both the numbers and the organisation of schools. The dissolution of the monasteries and other religious foundations in the reigns of Henry VIII and Edward VI provided the funds both for the foundation of a number of royal grammar schools (such as the King Edward VI School at Stratford) and for the acquisition of a large quantity of buildings which proved suitable for conversion. At the same time fresh sponsors were coming forward in the form of towns and merchants, as well as the church and wealthy individuals, while the curriculum was developing to take advantage of the new learning of the Renaissance; schools were also being divided into classes corresponding to the age and ability of the pupils.

The earliest school built to reflect these new influences was St Paul's School in London, founded in 1509 by John Colet, the Dean of St Paul's Cathedral in the City of London, to replace the school which had been attached to the cathedral from the twelfth century. The buildings were completed in 1512, and consisted of a single-storey school building flanked on either side by four-storey houses for the accommodation of the high master (for the first time a married layman, not a cleric) and the second master respectively. The school comprised four rooms: an entrance hall, where younger pupils received instruction in the Christian religion; a chapel; and two schoolrooms, divided by a curtain, for the instruction of the school's 153 pupils who were divided into nine forms. Those who boarded slept in dormitories on the upper floors of the staff houses. The buildings were destroyed in the Great Fire of London of 1666; St Paul's has subsequently moved to west London.

Education remained the privilege of a minority of children (most of them boys) until the late nineteenth century when the 1870 Education Act finally introduced the concept of education for all. Administration of the new system was placed in the hands of locally elected school boards of which the largest and most important was the London School Board. The LSB marked its establishment by holding an architectural competition for the design of an elementary school for 1,600 pupils. The competition was won by Professor Roger Smith, and the resulting Ben Jonson school in Bethnal Green, east London became the forerunner of the first generation of schools for all.

UNIVERSITIES

The town of Oxford originated as a village clustered round an eighth-century monastery founded by the Saxon Princess Frideswide, and prospered thanks to its site at a strategic ford across the River Thames on the borders of the Anglo-Saxon kingdoms of Wessex and Mercia. Royal councils met here in the eleventh century, and the Normans fortified the town with a castle. Oxford was therefore a secure and flourishing market town and already a centre of learning when, in 1167, English scholars were recalled from the University of Paris during a dispute between Henry II of England and Philip II Augustus of France, and returned across the Channel to settle there and create the first British university.

By the end of the twelfth century there was a substantial body of scholars in the town, studying for their degrees in the arts which were usually the basis for further study in theology. They lived in lodgings or monastic hostels, studied in hired halls and churches and were often at odds with the townspeople; after one riot in 1209 a part of the scholarly community dispersed to found the rival university of Cambridge. Oxford reconvened in 1214 under the protection of a papal charter giving it independence from the town.

The university colleges are self-governing communities within the university with their own statutes and funds, and the first ones emerged in the thirteenth century. In 1249 William of Durham left an endowment for twelve masters of arts to study theology, and the hall established for them eventually became University College, the earliest collegiate foundation of its kind in Britain — however, none of the present buildings dates from before the seventeenth century.

The oldest collegiate buildings in Britain are those of Merton which was founded in 1264 by Walter de Merton, the newly appointed Chancellor of England. Thirteenth-century relics include stonework in the main gate, the hall (first documented in 1277 and largely rebuilt in the 1870s), and the chapel which was started in 1290 but never completed; in its truncated form it had only the choir, crossing and transepts of a monastic church of the time, it did not have nave or aisles — it became the model for the peculiarly Oxonian type of college chapel. Mob Quad, Merton's first quadrangle, grew gradually in stages between 1308 and 1378.

In Cambridge, the earliest college was Peterhouse, founded sixteen years after Merton in 1280. Its scholars lived initially in hostels and the first building put up for the college itself was the hall of 1286.

The first college ever to have been planned and built from the outset as a single unity is New College, Oxford, whose foundation stone was laid in 1380. It was conceived by William of Wykeham, Bishop of Winchester, who established Winchester College as part of the same educational project (see above page 38), and was designed and built by William Wynford. The Great Quadrangle, the earliest to be designed as such in any university, was in place by 1386 complete with hall, chapel, library and rooms for both fellows and scholars to live in college. Future colleges at both Oxford and Cambridge followed the example of New College, whose design had the advantage of allowing for future additions — they could be grafted onto its living core.

The earliest building in Britain put up for specifically university purposes — as opposed to those of an individual college — is the Congregation House; this was built in the early fourteenth century onto the north side of St Mary the Virgin, the parish church of Oxford and the mother church of the university, whose ceremonies were held there until the completion of the Sheldonian Theatre in the seventeenth century. Begun at the expense of Thomas Cobham, Bishop of Winchester, the Congregation House served as the parliament and court of the university until the late fifteenth century; it is a vaulted stone chamber measuring 13.8 by 5.5m (45¼ by 18ft) and is now a chapel. Above, a room was built as the first home of the university library (see page 82, Libraries); it

is now a parish meeting room. The earliest teaching building at Oxford is the Divinity School, which was built over the period 1420–90. In Cambridge, the Divinity School is earlier and was completed by about 1400.

The oldest university in Scotland is St Andrews, founded in 1411, followed by Glasgow (1451), King's College, Aberdeen (1495), and Edinburgh (1583). The first degree-according institution in England and Wales after Oxford and Cambridge was St David's, Lampeter (founded in 1822) which was incorporated in 1971 into the University of Wales, a federal establishment created in 1893 from existing colleges set up in the 1870s and 1880s. University College, London, the oldest and largest college of the University of London, dates from 1826.

The Open University, created by royal charter in 1969, has neither full-time students nor minimum academic requirements — it provides courses for adults studying at home from its headquarters in Milton Keynes, Buckinghamshire and satellite offices throughout the country.

There are forty-eight universities in the UK.

Plate 13 Merton College chapel, Oxford. *(Thomas Photos, Oxford)*

EXCHANGES AND FINANCIAL MARKETS

The first specialised commercial building erected in Britain was the Royal Exchange in the City of London. It opened in 1569 to accommodate Britain's growing overseas trade and was built to the designs of a Flemish architect, Henryk van Paesschen, on the instructions of a prominent City merchant, Sir Thomas Gresham. Merchants like Gresham traded regularly with Antwerp, then the commercial centre of Europe, and their experiences of dealing with their opposite numbers in the Antwerp Bourse suggested forcibly that London was behind the times in having no equivalent place where local and overseas merchants could discuss their business in comfort and privacy rather than in the open street or taverns.

In 1566, therefore, Gresham (whose only son and heir had not long before died) offered to build London 'a Bourse for merchants to assemble upon', *if* a suitable site could be found. One was — between Cornhill and Threadneedle Street — and the land with the eighty houses standing on it was bought for £3,532, the sum being raised by a subscription to which twenty of the livery companies of City merchants contributed. The building was completed in 1568; it was designed in Flemish style and closely resembled the Antwerp Bourse — built in Flemish brick, it was a hollow square with an internal quadrangle surrounded by an arcade giving access to over one hundred shops which were let out as a means of paying for the building. After the death of Sir Thomas's widow, it was left in trust to the City Corporation and the Mercers' Company (one of the oldest livery companies of City merchants). It burned down, however, in the Great Fire of 1666.

Its replacement, which opened in 1669, was designed by Edward Jerman, one of the three surveyors appointed by the city corporation to oversee the reconstruction of the city, and it was described as 'the most beautiful, strong and stately building of its kind in Europe'. It, too, was destroyed in 1838 by a fire which broke out in a part of the building occupied by Lloyd's (see page 46) which had its headquarters there from 1774 to 1928. This time, the City committee responsible for rebuilding the Exchange decided to hold an architectural competition for the new building. The eventual winner was William Tite, appropriately enough the son of a merchant himself. Tite's third Exchange was completed in 1844 and opened by Queen Victoria, and reflects in its architecture the dawning age of Victorian civic and commercial confidence. The prominent classical portico and pediment at the front lead into an internal cloister which reproduces the layout

Plate 14 The west front of the present Royal Exchange with (left) the Bank of England building and (behind the bank) the tower of the Stock Exchange. *(Guardian Royal Exchange Assurance Group)*

of the first Exchange and is richly ornamented. The pediment shows the figure of Commerce flanked by traders from around the world.

For 250 years the Royal Exchange was Britain's most important commercial centre. From the early nineteenth century, however, the expanding volume of business of the Victorian era resulted in more buildings, to house the more specialised branches of business — the Stock Exchange (1802); the Coal Exchange (1849); the Wool Exchange (1874); these had their counterparts in major cities throughout Britain. Since 1720, the Royal Exchange has been a principal office of the Royal Exchange Assurance Company (from 1968, the Guardian Royal Exchange) which paid out for the total loss of the second exchange in the 1838 fire — a sum of £45,000. The inner courtyard was covered in 1880 with a glazed barrel-vaulted roof and dome; between 1939 and 1982 it had no commercial role, and served variously as a temporary museum, an exhibition area, and in 1953 as a theatre, its productions celebrating the coronation of Queen Elizabeth II — the first theatre to function within the boundaries of the City of London for over 200 years. In 1982 it became the home of the London International Financial Futures Exchange (LIFFE), one of the new generation of organisations set up to handle the increasingly complex business of global financial services. To preserve the interior LIFFE's architects created a prefabricated trading floor inside, but independent of, the Victorian cloister.

During its long history, the Royal Exchange has played host to several financial organisations, among them Lloyd's and the Stock Exchange, before these had buildings of their own. Lloyd's, the world's foremost market for marine and specialist insurance, began life in 1686 as a coffee house close to what were then London's docks. Run by Edward Lloyd, it was one of hundreds of such houses which had been springing up in British towns since the middle of the seventeenth century. Groups of merchants with common commercial interests used them as social and business centres, a tradition which survived for over 200 years, and Lloyd's was the most famous of them all.

Lloyd's customers, thanks to the location of his premises, were shipowners, sea captains and merchants, all concerned with chartering vessels to export or import goods, and Lloyd employed runners to bring up-to-date information from the docks on ship arrivals and sailings, cargoes and losses. Insurance had been available to traders since the fourteenth century and information of this kind was essential for arranging any insurance matter — it was not long, therefore, before Lloyd's became London's chief insurance market for covering marine risks. These were 'underwritten' by wealthy merchants, each taking a share of the premium and guaranteeing to pay a share of any loss; this underwriting system is still the principle of insurance today.

In appearance, Lloyd's remained a coffee house, with a counter at one end and tables and chairs at which patrons drank coffee and discussed business — the main indication of its commercial role was a 'pulpit' from which a waiter would announce important news. However, by 1774 Lloyd's had become an institution, and moved into the Royal Exchange. It progressively extended its activities beyond marine insurance, initially to fire and burglary cover, and by the 1920s had finally outgrown the Exchange.

In 1928, Lloyd's took possession of its first-ever purpose-built headquarters on the corner of Leadenhall Street and Lime Street. This was an historic site which had once been occupied by East India House, the office of the East India Company and the earliest commercial building ever put up in Britain for the use of a single business organisation (see page 103, Offices). Lloyd's first permanent home was designed by Sir Edwin Cooper, and its main internal feature was the underwriting 'Room'. In response to continuing growth in business, Lloyd's was extended across Lime Street in the 1950s and a new, larger Room created there. By 1977 Lloyd's had outgrown its premises again — for the third time in half a century — and its governing corporation therefore decided to plan a completely new headquarters, on the site of the 1928 building, and to accommodate both future expansion and the impact of the modern computing and information technology on financial services.

From an international shortlist Lloyd's chose as its architect Richard Rogers: Rogers' 'Centre Pompidou' was the newest landmark of Paris, and he intended to solve the accommodation problem by building flexibility into his design. The new underwriting room forms the base of a huge atrium under a glazed, barrel-vaulted roof; it is surrounded by twelve levels of galleries which open out into additional underwriting space as and when the needs of the international insurance business dictate — otherwise, these can be partitioned off as lettable offices.

Typically, large commercial buildings would have a single-service core housing lifts, environmental services and sanitary accommodation; but this was inappropriate at Lloyd's where, with a working population up to ten times greater than that of normal offices, more than one entrance was needed and a single core would have occupied too much valuable space. All the services are therefore grouped in satellite turrets hung on the exterior of the atrium, and serve also to break up what would otherwise have been a monolithic structure into a fragmented outline redolent of the towers and spires characteristic of the historic city. The new Lloyd's, which opened in 1986, is the most dramatic building in London this century, and in striking contrast to the humble coffee houses where the insurance market originated.

Like Lloyd's, the Stock Exchange originated with groups of merchants meeting in City coffee houses and operated, for a time, from the Royal Exchange. It moved to its present site in 1802, into a building designed by James Peacock and rebuilt in 1853 by Thomas Allason. This was demolished in 1967 and replaced by a 26 storey skyscraper completed in 1969 to the designs of two firms of architects, Llewelyn-Davies, Weeks, Forestier-Walker & Bor, and Fitzroy Robinson & Partners. Its central feature — as in previous designs — was the trading floor where brokers acted for investors (whether individual or corporate) and traded securities with the jobbers who dealt in them. It expressed, in other words, the long-standing City tradition of doing business face to face. The major banks, brokers, traders and insurers all operated from offices within walking distance of each other, and it was largely in order to maintain this historic concentration of business activity that, in the second half of the twentieth century, the City of London imitated Manhattan in rising skywards.

In October 1986, however, came the City's 'Big Bang' — the deregulation of the Stock Exchange in response to the increasingly international nature of the financial securities markets. Advances in communication technology meant that London could take full advantage of its geographical position midway between the time zones of New York and Tokyo, and trade with both in a single day. To exploit these new opportunities the Stock Exchange abolished the professional distinction between brokers and jobbers and allowed its member firms to trade from their own offices, where computers and VDU screens have now superseded the centuries-old reliance on personal contact. The modern successor to the trading floor of the Stock Exchange is the dealing floor of the new financial conglomerates formed by banks, brokers and jobbers. Thanks to the speed of modern communication, these can operate from buildings well away from the traditional heart of the City, in new financial districts such as Broadgate, near Liverpool Street Station, or Canary Wharf in the London Docklands. In one sense, the whole of the City and its surrounding areas now constitute a single vast exchange.

EXHIBITION CENTRES

In Paris, trade exhibitions were regular events by the middle of the nineteenth century — they had in fact been promoting French-produced goods with increasing success since 1798, during the burgeoning of national energy which the Napoleonic era inherited from the French Revolution. Across the Channel, with the Industrial Revolution in full spate and the advent of the railways in the 1830s providing a new means of distributing goods and extending markets, British manufacturers were looking for ways of displaying their own products and there was keen competition between London and Birmingham, the centre of the country's manufacturing industry.

The Society for the Encouragement of Arts, Manufactures and Commerce was founded in 1754 and later became the Royal Society of Arts. In 1847, it organised the first of a series of trade exhibitions in its London premises at no 8 John Adam Street, off the Strand. This house, completed in 1774 and still the society's headquarters, was designed and built for it as part of the redevelopment of the Adelphi (the name given to the area) by the Adam brothers, and included from the outset a large hall for displays. Prince Albert, the German-born consort of Queen Victoria, was an enthusiastic supporter of the idea of exhibitions and was elected as the society's president that year. Albert took a keen interest in technical progress and was anxious to play a useful role in the life of his adopted country. Also working with the prince was a particularly energetic member of the society, Henry Cole, an industrial designer and technical educationist who had been involved with Rowland Hill in introducing the penny-post in 1840 (see page 124, Post offices).

In 1849 the Society's third annual exhibition overflowed from the display hall into other areas of its building, and attracted over 100,000 visitors. On Cole's return from the most successful-ever French exposition held in Paris that same year, he and the Prince decided to stage a much more ambitious event two years later (to allow for the necessary preparation) and in a new location. The Prince decided that it should be open to foreign as well as British products — making this the first international exhibition ever held — and the anticipated scale of the project ruled out the use of the courtyard of Somerset House (see page 70, Government buildings) which the government had originally offered. In the absence of any other suitable building of the necessary size, the remaining solution was to build a purpose-designed exhibition hall on a site which it was eventually decided should be a 9ha (22 acre) plot in the southern part of Hyde Park.

While preparations for 1851 were under way, Birmingham stole a march on London with the opening of the first building to be completed specifically for exhibition use. Bingley Hall was built at a cost of £6,500 on the site of Bingley House, the family home of the banker and anti-slavery campaigner Charles Lloyd, in Broad Street — then a rural road running south-west from the town centre. The eighteenth-century brick-built house and the grounds in which it stood had been acquired by the Midland Railway who needed to tunnel beneath them so as to lay the main line to Wolverhampton and the Potteries; but before its demolition the property was used as the venue for the 1849 exhibition of the Manufacturers of Birmingham and the Midlands Counties, with temporary buildings put up to provide the extra space needed. The following year the organising committee of the Birmingham cattle show invited a local firm of builders, Branson and Gwyther, to build them a temporary exhibition hall on the now cleared site; however, the firm advised that it would cost little more to put up a permanent building which would be a sounder investment.

Branson and Gwyther gave the job of designing it to Julius Chatwin, a twenty-year-old draughtsman in their employment who later became a prominent Birmingham architect. Chatwin produced a Roman Doric design with external walls in red and blue brickwork and an interior of iron and glass. To have the building ready in time, Branson and Gwyther made use of materials which could be diverted from other contracts — bricks from a Birmingham railway viaduct, and iron columns from a proposed railway station. Opened in October 1850, with a circus as the overture to the cattle show which took place in December, Bingley Hall was the largest building ever put up in Birmingham, with a plan area of 68m by 64.5m (224 by 212ft) under a roof of 1,087sq m (11,700sq ft) of glass. It continued to stage exhibitions and shows until April 1984 when the final event, the 1984 International Custom & Sports Car Show, closed down; the following year Bingley

Plate 15 Bingley Hall, Birmingham, Britain's earliest (and now demolished) national exhibition building. *(City of Birmingham Library)*

Plate 16 The Crystal Palace after its move to Sydenham — from exhibition hall into Victorian leisure centre. *(London Borough of Bromley Library)*

Hall was demolished to make way, appropriately enough, for the Birmingham Convention Centre.

While Bingley Hall was already drawing crowds in Birmingham, the planning of the 1851 exhibition went ahead in London under the direction of a Royal Commission, headed by Prince Albert; in 1850 this had launched an international competition for the design of the exhibition building. However, the resulting 245 submissions were all rejected and the Commission's building committee, which included such eminent men as the engineers Robert Stephenson and Isambard Kingdom Brunel, and the architect Charles Barry, came up with an astonishing scheme of their own — a low, sprawling structure crowned by an enormous pudding-like dome which was over 61m (200ft) in diameter, larger than that of St Peter's in Rome. The derision which this provoked might have ended the entire project prematurely had it not been for Joseph Paxton.

Paxton began his career as a gardener's boy at the Royal Horticultural Society's gardens at Chiswick, west London. The society leased these from the Duke of Devonshire, who used to meet Paxton in the course of his strolls from his villa at Chiswick House — he was sufficiently impressed to appoint him, at the early age of twenty-three, head gardener on the Devonshire family estates at Chatsworth, in Derbyshire. At Chatsworth Paxton's work included the design and building of glasshouses, in which he became an expert. The largest of his creations in iron and glass was the Great Conservatory, completed in 1840 and covering 0.4ha (1 acre) of ground; and the most significant was the Lily House, built for a rare South American water plant which was failing to thrive in Britain. In Paxton's Lily House it flowered for the first time.

Paxton was by then a director of the Midland Railway and it was at a business meeting in London, just after the rejection of the competition entries, that he drew on his experience with glasshouses to sketch out a fresh idea on a sheet of blotting paper. This was shown to Henry Cole who promptly invited Paxton to prepare a detailed plan with costs; published soon after the Royal Commission's building committee's proposal it was received with enthusiasm which left the issue in no doubt. The commission approved the Paxton design on 15 July 1850, work began on the foundations in August, and the first iron column went up the following month on concrete foundations which still lie beneath the turf of Hyde Park; the building was completed in January 1851 in good time for opening of the Great Exhibition in May, and was the first modern, prefabricated structure in Britain.

The Crystal Palace, as it was soon being affectionately called, was really a gigantic greenhouse on three levels, made technically possible by recent improvements in glass manufacture and by the removal of onerous taxes on that material. Before 1830 the largest panes of good quality glass available were no more than 0.6 by 0.4m (24 by 15in), cut from circular discs of 'crown' glass; but in 1832 the Birmingham firm of Chance Brothers introduced into England the mass production of sheet glass, using the European cylinder process to turn out panes of up to 1.2 by 0.9m (4 by 3ft). Chance Brothers supplied 93,000sq m (one million sq ft) of glass for the Crystal Palace, most of it in panes measuring 1.2 by 0.25m (4ft by 10in).

The completed building was 563.5m (1,848ft) long by 124m (408ft) wide with a 22m (72ft) wide transept — this was an alteration to the original design, made so as to spare three large and well liked elm trees which duly survived as internal landscaping. Its iron frame weighed 4,500 tonnes. Inside, the 100,000 exhibits from countries around the world were displayed in four categories: raw materials, machinery, manufactures, and works of art. Over six million visitors came during the twenty-four-week run and the exhibition was a great financial success; it cleared a profit large enough to purchase 9ha (22 acres) of land immediately south of Hyde Park in south Kensington for the creation of an entire precinct of museums, colleges and cultural institutions (see page 98, Museums).

When the Great Exhibition finally closed on 15 October 1851, the immediate question was what to do with the Crystal Palace. When Parliament turned down Paxton's proposal to keep it permanently in Hyde Park as a winter garden, he formed a company to buy both the building and an estate at Sydenham in south-east London where he had it rebuilt, taking full advantage of its 'kit of parts' form of prefabricated construction to enlarge the structure, adding transepts and an arched roof. Opened in 1854 the reconstructed Crystal Palace was the first large-scale leisure centre with attractions for the whole family: there were permanent exhibitions of art and industry, a museum of natural history, an aquarium, a theatre and a concert hall capable of seating audiences of 4,000.

The central area was used for special exhibitions and shows (the first aeronautical exhibition in 1868, the first motor show in 1903), for gymnastic displays, boxing matches and similar events. The grounds were laid out with gardens and terraces, sports pitches, children's playgrounds, fountains — jetting 76m (250ft) high and supplied by specially built water towers — and lakes. The Crystal Palace attracted up to two million visitors a year, and gave its name to the London suburb which grew up round it.

By the early twentieth century, however, the great days of the Crystal Palace were past. It was suffering from financial and maintenance problems and only survived the bankruptcy of the company which owned it by being acquired for the nation in 1913. Attendances never regained their early levels, and the fire which destroyed the building in November 1936 at least ensured it a fittingly spectacular end. Rebuilding was impracticable because of the costs involved and the site was cleared in 1937, to lie empty until after World War II. In 1951, the centenary of the Great Exhibition, Parliament handed the site over to the then London County Council which was required to develop it for educational and recreational purposes. The result was the National Recreation Centre (see page 148, Sports centres).

The success of the original Great Exhibition prompted a whole series of Victorian exhibition halls and centres, although none was as dramatic as the Crystal Palace. The second international exhibition opened in 1862 in south Kensington, west London on land purchased from the profits of the Great Exhibition, in another building of cast iron and glass but less flatteringly nick-named the Brompton Boilers. The exhibition was overshadowed by the death of Prince Albert the previous year and was not a success, and the structure was re-erected in Muswell Hill, north London as the Alexandra Palace (see page 16, Broadcasting buildings). In 1887 the Empress Theatre Arena opened at Earls Court, west London; intended at first for circuses and similar performances, it was rebuilt as an exhibition centre in 1937 when it was, for a time, the largest building in Britain. White City was laid out in 1908 for the Franco-British Exhibition with a stadium which was the venue for the fourth Olympic Games held the same year. White City did not, however, survive World War I as an exhibition complex and much of the site is now occupied by the BBC.

None of the existing centres proved adequate for the needs of British industry as the country's economy recovered after World War II. Their deficiencies of size and flexibility were highlighted by the Festival of Britain, first suggested in 1946 by the Royal Society of Arts and staged in 1951 — the centenary year of the Great Exhibition — in specially designed temporary buildings on a site on London's South Bank. By the 1950s the British Industries Fair (BIF) was having to spread over three centres, two in London and one in Birmingham. The BIF came to an end in 1957 and when the Government subsequently asked the Federation of British Industry (FBI) — now the Confederation of British Industry — to advise it on the needs of British manufacturers, the FBI stressed the need for a modern exhibition centre to promote British exports. Over the next decade various venues were examined (including Crystal Place) but no decision had been reached when, in 1969, Birmingham took the initiative as it had done more than a century earlier.

In that year Birmingham City Corporation bought 121ha (300 acres) of farmland at Bickenhill, lying 13km (8 miles) south-east of the city centre and close both to the main London to Birmingham railway line and the West Midlands regional airport at Elmdon. Working jointly with the Birmingham Chamber of Industry and Commerce the city produced a feasibility study for a national exhibition centre to be located here, in the centre of the country with good rail, air and motorway access. The following year the Labour Government, which had decided as a matter of regional policy that Britain's new exhibition centre should be outside London, endorsed the Birmingham project.

Construction began in 1973 on a complex of exhibition 'hangars' — simple steel-framed envelopes clad in anodised aluminium, steel sheeting and precast concrete under a lightweight flat roof, with concrete floors of road quality to withstand the weight of exhibits, machinery and delivery vehicles. The buildings are standardised structures of their day, just as the Crystal Palace was in the materials that were then appropriate. The National Exhibition Centre (NEC) opened in 1976 with an initial six halls and offered a total display area of 92,900sq m (1,000,000sq ft); subsequent extensions have increased the overall capacity to 125,000sq m (1,345,000sq ft) of space. The designers were Edward D. Mills and Partners for the exhibition halls, and Richard Seifert and Partners for the site development, with Birmingham-based quantity surveyors Francis C. Graves and Partners project managers. The success of the NEC led to the proposal to build a complementary convention centre in the heart of Birmingham, on the site of Bingley Hall.

FACTORIES

Manufacturing began as a domestic activity, organised from home in the same way that agriculture still largely is. In medieval times most of the goods that people needed were produced either in their own homes or in those of craftsmen — weavers, carpenters, smiths and millers — who lived over or next to their places of work. All that was originally needed for production was space of no more than domestic size and scale, and other buildings were added as the need for them arose — for storage, for example, with the warehouse as the equivalent of the barn. External centres of production were few and far between. Among the most important were the monasteries; Bordesley Abbey, founded in 1148 in what is now Redditch, Hereford and Worcester produced iron-work; it is credited with the introduction of needle-making to the West Midlands, the earliest historical instance of the region's long association with metal manufacture.

The first industrial buildings as such were mills. Powered by natural energy sources such as animals or streams and rivers, these played a central role in the life of every community, grinding grain for flour to make bread (the staple diet of the population) and providing power for mechanical processes such as timber sawing and boring. The Domesday Book, completed in 1086, lists over 5,000 mills, most of them in the southern part of the country, and new emergent processes harnessed the same technology. So from the end of the medieval era, rag mills used water-powered shredding machines to produce pulp for making the paper which replaced parchment made from animal skins; and by the sixteenth century powder mills were grinding the elements of gunpowder, most of which had previously had to be imported, while the arrival of tobacco from America made snuff-grinding another application.

The construction and equipment of the early water mills was of the simplest kind. The building itself was a low shed of stone or timber, built beside or over a stream with a timber paddle wheel positioned in the current, its axle shaft passing through the wall of the mill to drive a grindstone or other machinery through a basic arrangement of gears and cogs. A good example is Alderley Old Mill at Nether Alderley, Cheshire, which was originally built in the fifteenth century and worked until the outbreak of World War II; it has now been fully restored by the National Trust. The mill was so common and essential a feature of life that it became the generic name for the much larger and more complex buildings which were put up to accommodate the explosion of manufacturing generated by the industrial revolution of the eighteenth century — though interestingly, their development was foreshadowed by events taking place in Britain's oldest major industry, textile production.

Plate 17 The Derby Silk Mill, Britain's oldest factory, as it appeared in the late eighteenth century. *(City of Derby Museums and Art Gallery)*

The emergence of the factory from its domestic origins can be traced very clearly from the design of the stocking knitters' and weavers' cottages of the seventeenth century and later in the north and west of England. The knitting frames and handlooms with which whole families earned their living needed light and space to operate, and so there evolved a special kind of 'weaver's cottage', with long rows of windows lighting upper-level workshops — these were sometimes communal. Weavers' windows can still be seen in the garrets of the silk weavers' houses built in Spitalfields (east London) by Huguenot refugees from France who came to Britain after the revocation of the Edict of Nantes in 1685. By the eighteenth century textile production was beginning to be centralised in workshops which were either converted from other uses — from houses, warehouses, barns or corn mills — or purpose built. Besides, the new machinery which was replacing the traditional spinning wheel was too large for cottage use and needed mechanical power.

The earliest purpose-built power-driven factory in Britain was the three-storey silk mill built in 1702 by Thomas Cotchett on an island in the River Derwent in Derby, the birthplace of silk throwing in Britain. Silk weaving was one of the most lucrative trades in the Britain of that time, thanks partly to the arrival of the Huguenots, and the River Derwent was a suitably powerful source of energy for driving the mill's single large water wheel. The mill was equipped with Dutch machinery and designed and built by George Sorocold, the greatest hydraulic and mechanical engineer of that period. Cotchett's enterprise unfortunately failed, but by 1721 Sorocold had built a larger and more successful mill alongside it for the brothers John and Thomas Lombe, who ran both. John Lombe had learnt the business working for Cotchett and had then gone to Italy, in order to study silk manufacture and machinery in the country where it was most advanced. By 1717 he was back in Derby with drawings of the machines in which he was interested and plans to build a mill of his own, using Sorocold's engineering skills.

The Lombe mill was of unprecedented size, the largest industrial building ever erected in Britain and one which was to be unsurpassed for the following half century. Like the machinery it housed, it was based on Italian models — the stair tower was Italianate in design and the mill is described as the 'Italian Works' in an inventory compiled by the owner who acquired it from Thomas Lombe's widow in 1739 (by this time, the property included the Cotchett mill). Built on stone foundation arches over the river the mill was 33.5m (110ft) long and 11.9m (39ft) broad and rose through five storeys to a height of 17m (55.5ft). The external walls were up to 0.46m (18in) thick culminating in battlements which concealed the heavy lead roof. Internal floors were supported on timber columns and lit by rows of tall windows, fourteen in each long elevation.

Daniel Defoe described the mill in his *Tour Through Great Britain*, first published in 1727. The fullest account appears in the posthumous fourth edition of 1748, and reads:

> Here is a curiosity of a very extraordinary nature and the only one of the kind in England; I mean those mills on the Derwent which work the three capital Italian machines [winding engines, spinning mills and twist mills] for making Organize [organza] or thrown [spun] silk, which, before these mills were erected, was purchased by the English merchants with ready money in Italy; by which invention one hand will twist as much silk, as before could be done by fifty, and that in much truer and better manner . . . One water-wheel gives motion to all the rest of the wheels and movements, of which any one may be stopped separately.

The Lombe mill was rightly regarded as the prototype of the modern factory with its size, production capacity and workforce of 300; it preceded Richard Arkwright's first cotton mill at Cromford, also on the Derwent, by fifty years and continued to produce silk under successive owners until 1908. Two years later, after being gutted by fire, it was rebuilt to approximately the same original dimensions but on only three storeys. In this form, and with some of the original stone foundation arches still visible, the building survives as the Derby Industrial Museum.

Early industrial buildings like the Lombe mill were rectangular structures close to streams or rivers with walls of loadbearing brick or stone; they were seldom more than 9m (30ft) wide because of their reliance on natural daylighting and were usually at least four storeys high, the number of machines which they could house effectively depending on the force of the water energy which could be harnessed. They were mostly built — like the foundries, factories and warehouses which were needed to house the booming industries of the eighteenth century — by local masons and millwrights; some were buildings of considerable dignity, the plain use of materials offset by regular fenestration and sometimes by architectural features such as pediments and cupolas, which were 'borrowed' from the domestic architecture of the time. Internally they were at first of timber post-and-beam construction, but this was too vulnerable to fire and by the end of the century, industrialists were exploring safer methods which took advantage of the new technology of cast iron.

The first completely iron-framed building in Britain was the brick-clad Benyon flax mill at Shrewsbury in Shropshire, which was completed in 1797. Designed by Charles Bage, this had a framework of cast-iron columns and beams which anticipated developments in structural frames in the following century when iron (both cast and wrought) was increasingly used to cover the large-span areas demanded by Victorian industry and commerce. During the last quarter of the nineteenth century, steel became widely and cheaply available and by 1910 steel frame construction was officially accepted in Britain as being adequate to support the weight of a structure, without relying on the external walls other than for enclosure. Reinforced concrete was another new structural material, and was first used in Britain in the Weaver and Company flour mills at Swansea, South Wales; these were designed by François Hennebique who had perfected the method in France. By this time it is evident that industrial buildings were possible of a scale and complexity undreamt of by the builders of the eighteenth-century mills and manufactories.

These pioneers had also been restricted to building on rivers, as had the builders of corn mills for centuries beforehand, because the flow of current (stronger and more consistent for industrial production in the Midlands and the North, than in the South) provided the only available source of continuous power to drive machinery until late in the eighteenth century. However, the evolution of the steam engine was to provide the next source of energy: fuelled by coal, it developed from its original function of pumping out deep mines to become a thermally efficient means of supplying rotary power. Factories could now be located wherever coal was mined or could be delivered — initially by canal and later (in the nineteenth century) by rail. New towns and cities emerged and with them, the great concentrations of industrial building which are commemorated as the 'dark Satanic mills' of William Blake's 'Jerusalem'. The German architect Schinkel, who visited Britain in 1826, recorded his impressions of Manchester's buildings: 'seven to eight storeys, as high and as big as the Royal Palace in Berlin'.

Electricity was to transform the first industrial revolution and become the driving force of the second (electronic) one; it was available as a power source from the late nineteenth century but only became the main source of energy for industry between the two world wars. Electrification — particularly after the creation of the National Grid in the 1930s — removed the last physical constraint on the location of factories and industrial plant; in future it was local and national planning policy which was to provide the geographical limitations, especially after the introduction in 1947 of the first Town & Country Planning Act. This introduced the legislative means to separate the residential, commercial and productive functions of society into defined categories and areas.

By the last quarter of the twentieth century, however, these divisions were proving too rigid — in the wake of the decline of heavy 'smokestack' industries and in face of the emergent 'sunrise' economy of electronic equipment and computer software, they were inappropriate. A new generation of workplaces has emerged to meet the needs of these modern, sophisticated production processes, providing interchangeable space for manufacture, research, administration and distribution. This convergence of office and production functions resulted in 'high-tech' buildings which, since 1987, have been enshrined in town planning legislation with the creation of a new 'B1' business category of buildings. Unlike the vast complexes needed for heavy industrial production, these are domestic in scale and in the comfort and quality of their working environments: in the electronic age, the workplace as 'home from home' is reversing the trend of two centuries.

Meanwhile the surviving eighteenth- and nineteenth-century mills have now, in their obsolescence, acquired the status of historic monuments. 'Nowhere in Britain' says the architectural historian Marcus Binney, referring to the textile mills of Yorkshire (mostly stone) and Lancashire (mostly brick), 'is there such an awe-inspiring collection of buildings proclaiming the sheer majesty of industry.'

The concept of the industrial town or village, with an enlightened industrialist building homes for workers near their place of employment, is generally associated with post-1850 developments such as Saltaire (Bradford, west Yorkshire) or Bournville (Birmingham, west Midlands). But the pioneer community in fact dates from two centuries before these: Whitehaven in Cumbria was founded in the 1660s by Sir John Lowther, a member of parliament and a contemporary of Sir Christopher Wren, whose wealth came from the west Cumberland coalfield. He planned Whitehaven as an extension to the tiny fishing harbour which his father had already expanded to export coal to Ireland.

Whitehaven is the earliest post-medieval planned town in England and covers an area of some 19ha (47 acres). Sir John laid it out on a rectangular grid pattern of streets, and drew up careful rules for the stone-built terraces which were to line them on the best principles of good estate planning. Each house, for example, was to be three storeys in height and 4.5m (15ft) wide. Unfortunately he sold his plots freehold and the occupiers were therefore able to sell off their gardens for housebuilding, which has played havoc with Sir John's enlightened vision. The grid-plan layout was adopted by Sir Titus Salt at Saltaire in 1850.

The nineteenth century witnessed the birth of another pioneering form of industrial development, the industrial estate. Trafford Park in Manchester had been the home of the de Trafford family since before the Norman Conquest, but by the end of the nineteenth century it had become a man-made island in a sea of commercial expansion. The first hint of its future role came as early as 1761 with the opening of the Bridgewater Canal; this was built to carry the Duke of Bridgewater's coal from his mines at Worsley, Lancashire to the centre of Manchester and followed an arc round the southern boundary of the de Trafford estate. By 1882 Manchester's future as a great manufacturing centre was under threat from competing port towns which were nearer to their overseas markets and sources of materials. Either the sea had to be brought to

Plate 18 The original British Ford factory at Trafford Park, the world's first industrial estate. *(Chris Makepeace)*

Manchester or Manchester's industries would go elsewhere, to the sea. In the event the sea came to Manchester — along the Manchester Ship Canal which opened in 1894, closely following the northern boundary of the park in its route to the city docks. Two years later, Sir Humphrey de Trafford decided that the time had come to sell out.

The new owners, Trafford Park Estates Ltd, transformed the 480ha (1,200 acres) of land into an industrial powerhouse with roads, railways, 600 houses for workers, and factories — as many as forty manufacturing companies set up during the first five years of its existence, and Trafford Park was the home of the first British factory built by the Ford Motor Company; even in the Depression of the 1930s more than 35,000 people were employed on the estate. Employment reached a peak of 75,000 during World War II, but began declining with the return of peacetime conditions. In 1987 the Trafford Park Development Corporation was set up with £160 million of government money to modernise one of the oldest working environments in the UK. Proposals were agreed for imaginative landscaping and a new water link between the two canals in an effort to bring the 'mother of industrial estates' up to the standard of its descendants nearly a century on — the modern business parks with their high quality of environment and architecture designed to attract 'high-tech' industries.

FORTRESSES AND MILITARY BUILDINGS

Defensive structures reflect the military technology which is available to attack them. The age of modern organised warfare began in the first millennium BC with the widespread availability of iron, which was used for the manufacture of weapons stronger and more durable than ever before and necessitated the development of defensible and strategically located fortresses.

By the ninth century BC, Britain's Celtic tribes were raising hill and promontory forts, choosing natural strongpoints which they reinforced with ditches and ramparts of earth or stone which rose as high as 12m (40ft) above the level of the ditch and were usually topped by a wall or timber palisade. Many of these forts became permanent settlements with populations of up to 2,000, while some in southern England, of the type described by the Romans as *oppida*, were large enough to accommodate an entire tribe — and therefore qualified as the first towns in Britain. One of the best known of these hill forts is Maiden Castle, a few miles south west of Dorchester, Dorset which covers an area of 20ha (50 acres). The Scottish equivalents were smaller and designed to protect a single family or group of families.

The age of hill forts came to an end with the Romans' final, successful invasion in AD43. They built their first permanent fortification at Richborough, on the Kent coast, and moved out from there to storm the hill forts and *oppida*. As they penetrated Britain, the Romans built forts of their own: initially of earth or turf and timber, and later of stone as they consolidated their rule — for example, along Hadrian's Wall which was put up between 123 and 133. Richborough was rebuilt in stone in the late third century as part of the defence of Britain against raiding Saxon pirates — the beginning of the end of Roman rule.

However, while it lasted, the interior of Britain was controlled from the great legionary fortresses of Caerleon, Chester and York, built in the 70s. Each of these covered an area of up to 24ha (60 acres) and housed 6,000 troops in long barrack blocks, together with hospitals, workshops and granaries within the defensive wall. A legionary fortress (*castra*) was laid out in a characteristic cross pattern with the two main streets intersecting at the command headquarters; a pattern which can still be seen in the ground plan of the City of Chester, whose name recalls its Roman military origins.

During the chaotic centuries following the final withdrawal of the Romans in the fourth century, the Britons and the successive waves of invaders who were fighting for control of the country simply made use of the Roman and pre-Roman forts or built their own versions. A later innovation was the *burh* ('borough') or fortified town, introduced by Alfred the Great as a protection against the Danes of the ninth century, the grid-like layout of which can still be seen in early towns like Wareham, Dorset and Wallingford, Oxfordshire.

The most dramatic step in defensive architecture came with the overthrow of Anglo-Saxon culture. Castles were the distinctive contribution of the Normans and became the mainstay of the pacification of England after 1066, but they were of a type completely alien to Britain, first devised in continental Europe as the private fortresses of local warlords following the break-up of Charlemagne's Holy Roman Empire. The Anglo-Saxons had seen nothing like them — they were the largest buildings to be constructed in Britain since Roman times, and contemporary commentators attributed William's triumph, as he rapidly consolidated his hold on his new country, to the natives' lack of any comparable means of holding land.

The Conqueror's forces built their first castle within weeks of their arrival in 1066. They had reinforced the Roman coastal fort of Anderida at Pevensey, where they landed, but Hastings Castle had to be ready before the defending forces of Harold II could arrive from the north of England where they had just routed a Viking invasion. The original Hastings Castle, the construction of which is depicted in the Bayeux Tapestry, was a prefabricated timber fort which William had made in sections in Normandy and ferried across the Channel with his invasion fleet. Built on a prominent cliff top overlooking the sea, it was the precedent of typical motte-and-bailey construction, with the keep (the fortified core) raised on an artificial earthen mound (the motte) and surrounded by the ditch or moat which had been excavated in the course of its construction. Outside was a courtyard (the bailey), protected by a defensive wall.

After William's decisive victory at the Battle of Senlac 9.5km (6 miles) inland, and his coronation in Westminster Abbey on Christmas Day 1066, Hastings Castle was rebuilt in stone. It was one of the most important Norman defences in the country, guarding the port which was used by the new dynasty to maintain links with its dominions on the other side of the Channel until King John lost them in 1204. Later in his reign this king, fearing a French attack, had the castle destroyed to prevent it being used as an invasion beachhead. Within a few years the castle was fortified again by Henry III but in 1287 storms cut away part of the cliff on which it stood and brought the keep crashing down into the sea, so ending the maritime role of Hastings. All that survive are ruins.

The Tower of London is Britain's oldest 'operational' castle, and is still in military (if largely ceremonial) occupation after 900 years; it was used for the detention of prisoners of war and the execution of enemies of the state of both world wars. As early as 1067 the Normans had built their first timber fortification on the site just east of the City of London, to control both its population and the River Thames which was the commercial lifeline of the city as it had been for centuries (see page 33, Docks). By 1078 the Conqueror had begun the rebuilding of the site as a great palatial and defensive complex of solid masonry. His architect was the Norman abbot Gundulf, Bishop of Rochester, whose claim to

the necessary experience lay in the ecclesiastical tradition of building in stone.

The chief and earliest of Gundulf's buildings is the White Tower which was completed around 1098. A massive structure of Kentish ragstone, reinforced with Caen limestone from Normandy, it is roughly square, measuring 36 by 32.5m (118 by 107ft) in plan, and rising 27.5m (90ft) above ground level. Inside it was divided originally into two storeys, the uppermost of which contained the Romanesque chapel of St John, and was galleried; it formed a residence for the king within which he could be perfectly safe from attack. During the sixteenth century this royal suite was subdivided to create the three storeys which are visible today. Further buildings were added during the twelfth century, and the complex which we know as the Tower of London had reached its definitive shape by the year 1300.

Hastings and the Tower of London were among the pioneers of more than 2,000 castles which had been built by the end of the twelfth century. The early ones were of timber or stone, depending on the materials available and the urgency with which they were needed, but stone soon became the prerequisite for permanent defences. The castle was also a prime administrative element in the feudal economy, forming the local power base of a Norman noble and enabling him to control the estates which he held through the favour of, and in return for loyalty to, the king, to whom he was pledged to give military support when needed. It was an instrument of domination, representing the peak of the art of fortification prior to the invention of explosives.

By the fourteenth century the great age of the castles was already beginning to pass. Militarily vulnerable to gunpowder, they also symbolised a division between invaders and invaded which had become obsolete, since they had merged socially and linguistically into a single people; furthermore the banning of private armies after the Battle of Bosworth in 1485 was another significant landmark proclaiming the arrival of settled conditions in the land. The Civil War of 1642–8 briefly restored their original role, with both sides acquiring and repairing strongholds; but once victorious, the protectorate of Oliver Cromwell 'slighted' many (to make them indefensible) and castles never again had any military significance in the history of Britain.

Those that survive have demonstrated versatility as well as durability by fulfilling a whole spectrum of functions. The Tower of London, once a visible statement of alien domination and a prison within living memory, has also served as a mint, an early museum (see page 94, Museums) and a menagerie (see page 163, Zoos); since being opened to the public in 1875 it has become London's most popular tourist attraction. A number of castles retained official roles, of the kind that began to develop during the Norman era. Chester, strategically sited on the borders of England and Wales, became a local seat of government soon after the Conquest and was rebuilt between 1788 and 1822

Plate 19 The ruins of Hastings Castle, the first post-Conquest Norman castle in Britain. *(Hastings Borough Council)*

as the administrative headquarters of the county of Cheshire, with a shire hall, court, gaol (replaced by the unattractive modern county hall) and barracks (now a regimental museum). Lancaster Castle remains a prison; Windsor Castle (see page 109, Palaces) is an official royal residence; four other castles are private homes and Dudley is a zoo. Leeds, Kent is used by organisations including the government as a residential conference and corporate hospitality centre, as well as being open to the public.

BARRACKS

Castles provided the obvious solution to the need for military accommodation during the centuries when men were enlisted for specific needs rather than serving on a permanent basis. The first standing army in Britain was established after the end of Cromwell's Commonwealth, and consisted of a regiment of foot guards and two troops of horse guards which were assigned to the protection of the restored King Charles II in his palace of Whitehall (see page 109, Palaces). To accommodate them, the Government put up the predecessor of the present Horse Guards building on the former tiltyard (tournament ground) of the palace. Completed in 1664 it provided stabling for horses on the lower floor, with rooms for the soldiers above. A century later the building was in poor structural condition, and was rebuilt to the designs of William Kent by John Vardy and completed in 1759. The new Horse Guards, stone faced with heavy rustication at ground-floor level, was a much larger and more ambitious affair; apart from stabling and accommodation for the soldiery, it contained offices for the Secretary of War, the Paymaster General, the Controller of Army Accounts and the Judge Advocate-General.

The building of barracks on a large scale began in Ireland following the capture in 1691 of the town of Limerick, which ended the attempt of the deposed James II to regain the British crown from William III. Ireland remained unsettled, however, and the government therefore decided to adopt a policy of quartering troops in strategic locations throughout the country, where they could be called on at short notice. Acts of Parliament passed in Dublin from 1697 onwards provided the necessary funds for a series of new barracks — to be built by the Corps of Royal Engineers — and the most important were those in Dublin. Commenced in 1705 and completed in 1709 at a cost of £22,863, the Royal Barracks in Dublin were designed to accommodate two regiments of infantry and three troops of cavalry. They were built in brick and stone, with stone-flagged floors and roofed with best Caernarvon slates. When completed they were regarded as the largest and most complete barracks in Europe, well in advance of anything that had previously been built in the British Isles. Their designer was Lt-Col Thomas Burgh, the Chief Engineer of Ireland from 1700 until his death. By 1717 nineteen barracks were under construction in various areas of Ireland; by 1746 there were seventy-three. The Royal Barracks were enlarged between 1776–93 but little altered thereafter.

In the following century the Crimean War focussed public attention on the accommodation of soldiers, and in 1857 the government appointed a Royal Commission to look into the sanitary condition of army buildings and the construction of military hospitals. The Commission's Report of 1861, after its members had visited virtually every barracks in the UK, provided the foundation stone of modern standards of barrack design and construction. It recommended, for example, that each soldier in a barracks should enjoy 17cu m (600cu ft) of space, while inspection showed that soldiers in some barracks were currently enjoying less than 7cu m (250cu ft) per man.

GOVERNMENT BUILDINGS

Today's government ministries and departments of state have their origins in what were once specific concerns of the royal household and its attendant court — the most important being money, without which no king could govern. Under the Anglo-Saxons the city of Winchester in Hampshire rose in status from being capital of Wessex to capital of England, and the *Anglo-Saxon Chronicle* records the existence there of a *madme hus* — a treasure house, or repository of the king's treasure; this would make it the most ancient building in post-Roman Britain to be recorded as having a specific governmental function.

It was situated in the old royal palace in the centre of the city beside the cathedral, having been there from time immemorial. The historian William of Malmesbury, writing of the accession in 1087 of William II Rufus, recounted how he hurried down to Winchester from his coronation at Westminster to examine his financial inheritance, and described the *madme hus* as containing 'all the treasure accumulated at Winchester through all the years of the kingdom'. By 1100 the treasure had been moved to the Norman royal castle at the south-west corner of the walled city, and this was not supplanted as the seat of the treasury until the 1180s, when first the Tower of London and soon afterwards the palace of Westminster took on this role.

Even before the end of the Anglo-Saxon era, however, the centre of government was beginning to shift to London, the most powerful city in Britain and a major port and *entrepôt* since the first century AD (see page 33, Docks). The Danish King Cnut built a palace at Westminster in the early eleventh century and both Harold II, the loser of the Battle of Hastings, and William the Conqueror were crowned in Edward the Confessor's newly rebuilt Abbey next to it. The permanent rôle of Westminster at the heart of the nation's affairs was confirmed by the erection of significant governmental buildings — Westminster Hall by William II and, under Henry II in the second half of the twelfth century, a new, two-storeyed exchequer office of stone construction — and the administration of British government has remained here ever since.

Westminster Hall, the oldest surviving government building in Britain, was planned as the main administrative and ceremonial centre of the kingdom; at 73m (240ft) long and 20.5m (67½ft) wide it was the largest building in the country, and was intended, like other Norman works, to demonstrate the power of the new régime — it also cost a great deal of money in unpopular taxes. Even so, the king was not satisfied when it was completed in 1099, describing it as 'a mere bedchamber compared with what I had intended to build'. As originally constructed, the hall was a great stone barn with an upper gallery of Romanesque arches and a roof supported on timber columns. It played a prominent rôle in national life (Simon de Montfort's Great Parliament met there in 1265) and in acknowledgement of its importance, Richard II had the Hall rebuilt on a grander scale in the late fourteenth century by Henry de Yevele, the most famous master mason of the period; he enlarged the windows and removed the original columns to create a clear, light internal space — although evidence of the original construction does still remain — and his fellow craftsman Hugh Herland made the magnificent oaken hammerbeam roof, weighing 600 tonnes, which is the finest and earliest of its kind in northern Europe.

From the thirteenth until the eighteenth century Westminster Hall was the centre of legal activity in England and Wales and the venue for some notable trials, including those of Sir Thomas More in 1535 and of Charles I in 1649. In the seventeenth century the Courts of Chancery and the King's Bench sat at one end of the Hall behind flimsy partitions — replaced in 1739 by a Gothic screen — and the Court of Common Pleas at the other. Two years later, in recognition of the growing inadequacy of the Hall, this last court moved into

Plate 20 Interior of Westminster Hall, in its time a centre of government and a court house. *(Crown copyright, reproduced with the permission of the Controller of HMSO)*

a new building immediately outside, and in 1754 the government sanctioned a new 'stone building' designed by John Vardy to house legal records and other official documents. In 1820 the courts still in the Hall had to be cleared for the coronation banquet of George IV — the first for sixty years — and the government decided that the only solution to the problem was to provide new purpose-built courts along the western wall of the Hall. Designed by Sir John Soane and opened in 1826, the new courts — all top-lit by skylights and clerestoreys — became a model for the future planning of legal buildings.

Within a decade of completion, however, these were also proving inadequate and the new courts which were needed to handle the growing volume of legal business were having to find temporary homes away from the historic legal precinct of Westminster Palace. In 1865 Parliament approved the building of a new set of civil courts in London — by which time cities such as Liverpool and Manchester had splendid court buildings of their own. The chosen London site was in the Strand, and the winner of the ensuing design competition was George Edmund Street who completed his Gothic composition in 1883; Soane's courts were demolished soon afterwards. Westminster Hall was spared in the fire of 1834 and remains as the largest Norman hall and the oldest complete royal building in Britain. It is now used for great state occasions.

Less altered as an ancient survival is the three-storeyed Jewel Tower which can still be seen in largely original condition, with external walls of Kentish ragstone — though these were stripped of their medieval decoration in 1719 — and, internally, an unrestored fourteenth-century ribbed vault. It was completed in 1366, situated at the far south-western corner of the Palace of Westminster as a secure depository for the personal treasure of Edward II; the designer, again, was Henry de Yevele. The Jewel Tower was a storehouse for government records from 1621 until 1864, when the Victoria Tower was completed in the new Palace of Westminster and took over the rôle. In 1869 it became the office for weights and measures administration; since 1938 it has been cherished as a national monument.

Government remained close to the court until the end of the seventeenth century. Following a fire in 1512, the royal palace had moved northwards from the environs of the Abbey to Whitehall — a name now synonymous with government in Britain — leaving the Palace of Westminster to become the preserve of parliament, which is still officially known by that name. Holders of court and government posts carried out their duties either in the Palace or from their own houses nearby; at Whitehall Palace, for example, the western side was devoted to government offices. These survived the fires of the 1690s which drove William III to look further west for his residence (see page 110, Palaces); the Treasury — as always the most important department of state — remained in place in a new building completed in 1736 and formed the nucleus of the future Whitehall government precinct which took shape over the next two centuries on the site of the abandoned palace.

At the same time, much of the work of government continued to be carried out from the town houses of statesmen, a tradition which endured from the Middle

Plate 21 The north block of Somerset House, the first purpose-built government office complex. *(Courtauld Institute of Art Fund)*

Ages into the nineteenth century. Westminster and Whitehall were attractive places to build, close not only to the court but to the river which offered a superior mode of travel to the roads. The best-known surviving example of a private house being used for government purposes is no 10 Downing Street, the official residence of the Prime Minister since 1732; it is formed from two houses erected in 1682–3 as part of a speculative development. Even the purpose-designed Admiralty of 1726 was planned primarily as a residential building, with spacious accommodation for the Lords of the Admiralty but only a single boardroom from which to run the Royal Navy.

By the middle of the eighteenth century, however, the administration of Britain's parliamentary democracy had outgrown the capacity of both Whitehall and Westminster and was scattered in a multiplicity of buildings across London from

Mayfair to Tower Hill. The government of the day accordingly began looking for a better solution. The opportunity presented itself in the form of Somerset House in the Strand, the mid-sixteenth-century riverside palace of 'Protector' Somerset, regent of Edward VI who was the short-lived heir of Henry VIII. A government report of May 1774 indicated that the building, which was designated as the Queen's official dower house, was falling rapidly into ruin. Within weeks, King George III had agreed to accept Buckingham House (see page 110, Palaces) as the dower house instead, and allowed Somerset House to be pulled down and its 2.5ha (6 acre) site 'employed for the purpose of building such offices as may be necessary and convenient for the public'.

The first government centre in Britain, and one of the first in the world, therefore, rose in its place — an innovatory building designed specifically to accommodate distinct government departments and institutional bodies in a single structure. The architect was Sir William Chambers, Britain's most distinguished official architect after Sir Christopher Wren, and he spent the last twenty years of his life on this project. Behind the Palladian front to the Strand Chambers he built a great collegiate-style quadrangle, 107 by 94m (350 by 308ft). The advantage of this arrangement was that it provided a separate entrance for each of the departments which were to be accommodated: the Navy Board, the Exchequer, the Stamp Office, the Lottery Office, the Hawkers' and Pedlars' Office, and the Duchy of Cornwall. In the 'Fine Rooms' of the Strand range were the meeting and exhibition rooms of three great learned institutions of the day — the Royal Academy, the Royal Society and the Society of Antiquaries; these moved to Burlington House, Piccadilly in the 1870s.

Somerset House was finally completed in 1800 after Chambers' death, by James Wyatt who was his successor as Surveyor-General (chief government architect). It was the largest publicly-financed construction project of Georgian Britain, costing £462,323, and was Britain's equivalent of the Uffizi ('Offices') in Florence, Europe's earliest 'government centre'. The Uffizi was the first office block to be erected for commercial or governmental purposes in the modern world, and was built between 1560 and 1571 for Duke Cosimo I de' Medici to house the administrative and judicial offices of his city-state, which at that time covered most of the Italian province of Tuscany.

Part of Somerset House remains in use as government offices to this day. However, in December 1987 the government granted the Courtauld Institute of Art of London University a hundred-year lease of the north block as its headquarters. The Fine Rooms on the first and second floors have been restored by the institute as a new public gallery for the display of the Courtauld collection, with its impressionists and post-impressionists, while the remaining areas serve as the offices of the institute and of its research library of the history of art. Both parts of Somerset House are, therefore, now fulfilling their original function for the first time for over a century.

The nineteenth century witnessed a spate of government office building in Whitehall. The 'government centre' approach of Somerset House was repeated in the building known as the 'Old Public Offices' between Downing and King

Charles Streets, which was designed to accommodate four distinct departments of state; three of these have merged to give the present-day sole occupant, the Foreign and Commonwealth Office. The building was constructed between 1862 and 1874 to the designs of George Gilbert Scott and Matthew Digby Wyatt in an Italianate style.

The successors of Somerset House and the Old Public Offices are individual ministries rather than multi-departmental buildings, which proved increasingly incapable of containing the relentless expansion of the administration. The accommodation needs of present-day government now spread well beyond their traditional location, but the Whitehall precinct remains one of the best and least-damaged assemblies of major historic buildings in Britain. This is thanks to the rejection by the government of the day, after a public outcry, of a 1960s plan for a new government precinct in Whitehall. Official policy swung from demolition and redevelopment to conservation and modernisation, and Whitehall has since become the subject of a thoroughgoing restoration programme.

HOSPITALS

The origin of the hospital, as its name suggests, lies in the ancient concept of hospitality as a social duty involving helping those in need. Travellers, pilgrims, the poor, the sick, the aged and the infirm all needed shelter and care, and it was a recognised obligation on royalty, the church and wealthy individuals to make provision for them. The earliest hospitals were invariably run by, or as part of, religious foundations such as abbeys or monasteries, where the inclusion of a guest house for travellers and an infirmary for sick monks were essential elements in the planning of the community. The earliest surviving monastic infirmary building is at Canterbury, and dates from the first years of the twelfth century.

Hospitals of this kind were simple in plan and construction. They were usually built of stone and were often single-storeyed, consisting of a single large hall (sometimes divided into aisles) with a chapel or altar at one end. Here the inmates lived, ate, slept, worshipped — and were looked after to the extent of current knowledge. An area would be set aside for the sick, but the medical skills available to them embraced little more than the application of herbal remedies and the performance of simple operations. The emphasis was on caring as much as on curing, and no doctors were employed before the fourteenth century. Special accommodation was obviously needed for patients who were suffering from contagious diseases such as leprosy, a widespread hazard in the Middle Ages, and the plague, which became a recurrent fact of life in Britain from the mid-fourteenth century. The Tudor St James's Palace (see page 109, Palaces) was built on the site of the lazar house (leper hospital) of St James in the Field, which John Stow, in his *Survey of London*, dates 'before the time of any man's memory', although it is first recorded in the late twelfth century in the reign of Henry II.

The earliest hospital in Britain whose history we can trace is St Peter's in York. It was traditionally founded in 937 by Athelstan, the grandson of Alfred the Great and the first king to claim rule over the whole of Great Britain, when he returned from his great victory over the Scots and Danes at Brunanburh in south-west Scotland. The king gave the canons of York Minster — the predecessor of the Norman cathedral — a piece of land near the Roman wall and endowed it, so they could build a hospital for travellers, pilgrims and other needy people. William II and Henry I both gave money and materials for extensions; in 1155, after being severely damaged by fire, the hospital was refounded by King Stephen and rededicated to St Leonard.

By the fourteenth century it was the largest establishment in the country, with over 200 inmates who were too sick or poor to support themselves, and with more than twenty children in care in an orphanage; but its role ended in 1537 with the dissolution of the monasteries under Henry VIII. The visible remains include the ruins of an annexe in Museum Street and, below the Theatre Royal, portions of a vaulted undercroft — both dating from the twelfth-century rebuilding. Excavation of the undercroft suggests that the hospital above was at least 29m (95ft) long by 16m (53ft) wide, and laid out as a single large chamber. The rest of the site is now occupied by St Leonard's Place, a terrace of late Georgian town houses on four storeys, built between 1834 and 1842 and currently used as offices by the City Council.

The oldest-established hospital in Britain today and the first to achieve a degree of independence from monastic control is St Bartholomew's, which still occupies the same site in the City of London — although its accommodation was originally no more sophisticated than St Peter's. It was founded in 1123 by Rahere, a cleric and courtier of Henry I, who was possibly the master of ceremonies in charge of royal entertainments. Rahere fell ill with malaria during a pilgrimage to Rome and vowed that, if he returned safely, he would found a hospital for the poor and sick of the City of London. He duly recovered in a monastic hospital on an island in the River Tiber which was dedicated to St Bartholomew. To fulfil his promise, Rahere obtained from Henry I a grant of land at Smithfield, then outside the boundaries of the City of London. The site was poorly drained ground used for tournaments, for the execution of criminals and for horse fairs and markets, the best known being Bartholomew Fair which was held each summer outside the gates of the hospital till 1855.

Plate 22 The Square of St Bartholomew's Hospital, London, in 1870. *(St Bartholomew's Hospital)*

Rahere's great design involved building a hospital and a priory which would be run by Austin Canons, a recently established religious order. The choir of Rahere's priory church survives as St Bartholomew the Great, and is one of the most important Norman buildings in Britain. Both buildings were consecrated in 1129 with Rahere becoming the first prior; but in 1170 his successor placed the hospital in charge of a layman, so securing it significant independence. Rahere had built his hospital for the indigent sick, but it soon developed into a major charitable foundation caring for orphans, abandoned infants and the aged, besides providing a night shelter for the poor. The *Book of the Foundation of St Bartholomew* describes it as being 'made of comely stonework'. From seventeenth-century plans and drawings, made when the medieval buildings were still standing, it is clear that they had grown in a pattern of squares and precincts round courts and gardens — as a community, in other words, rather than as an institution. The boundary to Smithfield was flanked by tenements of shops with living quarters above which were rented out to help finance the costs of running the hospital.

Of the medieval buildings, only pieces of twelfth-century masonry have survived; these were re-used in the tower of the hospital church of St Bartholomew the Less when this was rebuilt in the fifteenth century (the octagonal church itself is nineteenth century). It was originally one of five chapels which were built at various times to serve the foundation; it became a parish church during the Reformation with a parish virtually identical with the boundaries of the hospital, of which it continues to be the religious centre. (The other chapels were all demolished.) As a monastic foundation St Bartholomew's — in common with other hospitals — faced an uncertain future during the dissolution of the monasteries which began in 1536. However, it was one of the few to be saved, thanks largely to pressure from the City of London, and was refounded in 1544 by Henry VIII. The king's role is commemorated in the statue of him which stands over the hospital's new north gateway, designed and built in 1702 by members of the Strong family of master masons who had worked with Wren on St Paul's (it was rebuilt in 1834).

By the beginning of the eighteenth century the medieval buildings and subsequent additions (some of them of timber construction) were in poor structural condition and proving expensive to maintain — the new gate heralded a complete rebuilding on which the hospital governors decided to embark in 1713, following the example of other, less venerable medieval foundations. Their chosen architect was James Gibbs, a Scots-born and Italian-trained designer of City churches and country houses who had recently been elected a governor. Gibbs' approach was to sweep away the medieval buildings and replace them with a great square measuring 61 by 49m (200 by 160ft), laid out behind St Bartholomew the Less, its sides flanked by four dignified detached buildings in the Palladian style. These were built between 1730 and 1769 as funds became available, and were constructed of bricks made from Kentish clay and faced with stone — initially Bath stone (St Bartholomew's is one of the earliest examples of its use in London) and later the more durable Portland stone.

The north wing, completed first in 1732, was built as the administrative centre of the hospital, with offices for clerks and rooms for the admission, examination and discharge of patients on either side of the main carriage entrance. Above all it was designed quite deliberately to impress philanthropically minded members of society whose benefactions were needed to pay for the planned ward blocks which would complete the square and form the actual hospital. No effort or expense was therefore spared on the Great Hall which is entered at first-floor level up the grand staircase. The Hall, double-height below an ornate coffered ceiling, is still used for celebrations, receptions and recitals. Its walls are virtually covered with panels and tablets listing past benefactors whose generosity has amply justified the trouble taken over its design.

The staircase is flanked by two paintings by William Hogarth who is better known as a caricaturist; they were his contribution to the fund-raising. The more striking is of Christ at the Pool of Bethesda healing the sick: around him, graphically portrayed, are sufferers from diseases typical of those being treated in the hospital in the eighteenth century — from rickets and cretinism to cancer and syphilis. Hogarth is credited with having used real patients as models, and professors at the hospital's medical school (St Bartholomew's has been involved in medical teaching since the eighteenth century and acquired its first purpose-built lecture theatre in 1795) have been known to begin their courses at this picture, with students being invited to identify the disease from the symptoms illustrated.

The other three wings, completed in 1740 (south), 1752 (west) and 1769 (east) were ward blocks — but all were designed in the same dignified style to create a setting as distinguished and timeless as that of an Oxford or Cambridge college. These blocks were initially of three storeys (attic extensions were added later) with four wards per floor, each of fourteen beds, making the total capacity of the hospital just over 500. The wards were grouped in pairs on either side of a cross corridor and separated by dividing walls with open fireplaces — so they were ventilated on one side only. At the ends of each floor were the staircases and private rooms for the nurses.

The east and west wings remain substantially as they were built (with the addition of lifts), but the south was replaced in 1935 by the George V medical block. This conceals a large group of buildings behind an elevation to the central square which, while taller than the original wings, sets out to complement them. The square, despite its gardens being sacrificed for nurses' shelters, remains one of the great setpieces of British architecture although, at the time, the layout had a serious medical purpose, reflecting the contemporary principle of building or rebuilding hospitals in detached blocks in order to reduce the risk of cross infection.

This arrangement became standard during the following century, and the logical development was the pavilion plan; this was first adopted in the Stonehouse Royal Naval Hospital in Plymouth, Devon, and completed in 1765, over fifty years after Wren had produced a never-executed pavilion plan for the naval hospital at Greenwich. Its wards could accommodate up to 1,250 patients in total, and were grouped in three-storey pavilions separated by low service blocks and connected by a covered arcade around a great court. Stonehouse was admired as being the most advanced hospital in Europe. Its wards were also the first which were designed to be self-ventilating, following observations of the superior recovery rates of military personnel being treated in temporary accommodation such as draughty tents and barns. The architect was Alexander Rouchead.

Florence Nightingale was the founder of the nursing profession; she published her *Notes on Hospitals* in 1858 after her experiences in the Crimean War of 1854–6, and produced her own specifications for what came to be known as the 'Nightingale Ward': 9m (30ft) wide and 4.8 to 5m (16 to 17ft) high, with windows on both sides. The first hospital built entirely under her supervision was the Royal Herbert military hospital at Woolwich, south London which was completed in 1865 under the supervision of Captain Douglas Galton, Florence Nightingale's nephew; it remained in military use until the 1970s. 'Nightingale Wards' continued to be built and used as the basis of pavilion-type hospitals in both Britain and North America well into the twentieth century; by which time economics dictated the adoption of more concentrated plans, with wards tiered in multi-storey blocks.

INNS AND HOTELS

Inns have existed for as long as people have needed to travel. The monasteries recognised the duty of hospitality to pilgrims and travellers, and these would be sheltered in a guest house and provided with food from the community's kitchens and drink from its own brewhouse. Outside monasteries, inns emerged in towns and along roads at convenient points such as crossroads, ferries and village centres, and some of them will have been of Saxon or possibly even earlier origin. There are lively references to inns in the literature of the fourteenth century; in the Prologue to his *Canterbury Tales*, Chaucer depicts his pilgrims assembling and dining at the Tabard Inn in Southwark, south London, while his contemporary Langland paints a lively scene in his *Vision Concerning Piers Plowman*, when Gluttony is diverted from his good resolution of going to church by the hostess of an inn where he spends a riotous evening. From time to time, evidence of over-indulgence stirred the authorities to action and in 1604 an Act of Parliament recognised inns, taverns and alehouses as places for 'the receipt, relief and lodging of wayfaring people travelling from place to place . . . and not meant for the entertainment and harbouring of lewd and idle people to spend and consume their money in lewd and drunken manner'.

Among inns of unquestionably early origin are the Trip to Jerusalem at Nottingham, which is hollowed out of the rock on which Nottingham Castle stands, and the Angel and Royal at Grantham, Lincolnshire. The Angel (as it was originally called) enters history as a pilgrims' inn and hostel of the order of Knights Templar, founded about 1118, who forfeited it to the Crown in 1308. The inn was much favoured by royalty; King John held court here in 1213, and it was at the Angel that Richard III — who reigned briefly from 1483 to 1485 — signed the death warrant of the Duke of Buckingham. The front of the Angel is enhanced by an oriel window overhanging the central archway, and has been described as a 'poem in stone'; most of its existing buildings are of fourteenth- and fifteenth-century construction.

Inns were the predecessors of the hotels and restaurants of today though at a fairly basic level of provision, and this remained the standard until well into the nineteenth century. Privacy and comfort were sparse; most travellers not only ate, but slept communally and private rooms were both rare and expensive. At the same time, as Derek Taylor and David Bush point out in their *Golden Age of British Hotels*: '. . . the best were amongst the most important commercial buildings of their time'. They were convenient venues where craftsmen and merchants could meet to discuss their affairs and complete business transactions (as in the later coffee houses — see page 46, Exchanges). They were the first sports clubs — many cricket and football teams began playing on fields close to inns. They were the only possible choice as the first post offices and, with the development of communications in the eighteenth century, became the 'stations' for the growing network of stage coach services. However, after 1830 when the passenger railways were coming into force, the rôle of the staging inns rapidly disappeared and by the spring of 1848 the last of the London-based mail coaches had made its final run. Some of these inns closed, some were taken over as railway stations and some continued to serve the local populace as taverns. At the same time, new needs were emerging for travellers who were becoming both more numerous and more demanding in the standards of accommodation which they required.

The early years of the century had already seen the opening of a superior kind of inn, mainly in converted town houses in London and other cities; it was quite distinct from that serving the coach industry, and expressed its refinement by the use of the French term 'hotel', setting out to serve the more fashionable visitors who had come to town or to spas and resort centres such as Brighton and Cheltenham. The best-known name from this period is Claridges which was founded in 1812 by a Frenchman, Joseph Mivart, in a small Georgian house in Brook Street, Mayfair. One source suggests that he was sponsored by the Prince Regent, who would have needed a well-run and discreet house in London to indulge the less public side of his life. Mivart began to develop his business in 1817, first taking over a second house in Brook Street and later expanding into five adjoining properties during the 1830s. By 1827 his establishment was patronised by the diplomatic corps, and by the early 1850s its guests included royalty.

In 1854 Mivart retired and his hotel was acquired by William Claridge who had not long before taken over a neighbouring hotel; he gave the amalgamated business his name. It continued independently until the last years of the nineteenth century, when competition from a new generation of purpose-built hotels made rebuilding a prerequisite of survival. In 1893 Claridges was acquired by the Savoy (which opened in 1889 and was a good example of the new competition), and rebuilt on the site in Brook Street where it stands today. One surviving example of an early nineteenth-century hotel is Browns in Dover Street, Mayfair, which was opened in 1837 by a retired manservant.

TRANSPORT HOTELS

The expansion of the mainline railways, which reached London in 1837 (see page 140, Railway stations), brought the need to accommodate travellers at their main terminals and junctions — and so the railway hotel was born. The first hotel which was built specifically to cater for railway passengers was the Bridge House at the south end of London Bridge, conceived at the same time as the terminus but developed independently. The architect, George Allen, produced an elaborate classical building in Portland stone which was considerably more impressive than the original station itself. The hotel opened in 1839 and survived until the 1960s.

Euston was the first hotel built by a railway company as part of a terminus

Plate 23 The main front and side elevation of the Midland Hotel, Derby, in the early years of this century. *(Photograph by W. W. Winter Ltd, established 1867, Derby, and reproduced with their kind permission and that of Midland Hotels Ltd)*

development. In fact there were two hotels which were built as a pair and completed in 1840 by Philip Hardwick (the architect of the station itself), one on either side of the great Doric portico. The hotels, each of five storeys, were designed to serve two different classes of guest: The Victoria, the western block, functioned as a bed-and-breakfast establishment, while The Adelaide (later The Euston) opposite was a conventional hotel. The two were joined together in 1881 by a bridge block and continued in use until the demolition of the Euston buildings in the 1960s.

The earliest surviving hotel built as part of a station complex is The Midland at Derby, which was completed in 1840 and designed as a whole with the original Trijunct station by Francis Thompson, the architect to the North Midland Railway, on an area of watermeadow called the Holmes to the south-east of the town centre. Thompson made the most of the hotel's location on what was then the edge of the town by designing it on an 'H' plan as a country house, with its main entrance looking away from the station and the

Holmes serving as its 'grounds'. The Midland Hotel survived the rebuilding of the station and is Britain's oldest purpose-built railway hotel still in operation, although it has passed out of railway ownership into the hands of a private company who have maintained its qualities while modernising the facilities. Together with a terrace of railway cottages, also by Thompson, the hotel forms the centrepiece of a conservation area commemorating the history of Derby as a railway and industrial city.

The earliest surviving railway hotel in London is The Great Western Royal Hotel which forms the front to Paddington station. Built in 1853, it was designed by Philip Charles Hardwick, the son of the architect of Euston station, in a heady mixture of styles, and was intended as a particularly sumptuous place to stay for the Great Western Railway's more prosperous clientele, who came from the affluent towns and landed estates of the Thames Valley and the Cotswolds.

RESTAURANTS

Like travelling, eating out became much more widespread and popular during the nineteenth century. Until the 1850s, however, restaurants were rarities run by Frenchmen and Italians and, while gentlemen had their clubs, most people who ate out did so as a matter of necessity rather than pleasure, in coffee houses and dining rooms which were laid out in a characteristic pattern, with rows of partitioned-off compartments running along either side of a long room. Inside these compartments diners (virtually exclusively male) ate at tables with room for up to six at a time; women and children patronised the small number of establishments which provided private rooms, or went to the baker's and the confectioner's.

Prevailing conditions were graphically illustrated by the *Building News* which, in 1857, campaigned for better restaurants and even anticipated their tourism potential by calling for them to be located on the upper storeys of buildings with balconies from which visitors could see the sights of the city. It criticised the typical level of provision where

> even in those houses where the meat is good, and the dinner quickly served, the rooms are, with few exceptions, low and straitened and the guests crammed together on inconvenient benches or equally uncomfortable chairs, the American ordinance of quick eating or gobbling being a necessity.

A correspondent, Henry Lennox, described the experience of a typical diner out:

> You enter a narrow doorway, say two feet [0.6m] wide and you stand in the 'dining house', a room some 20 by 15ft [6.1 × 4.5m], with a low dirty ceiling which seems to exhale the opaqueness that pervades the whole room. Six small narrow 'boxes' on either side of the room, fitted up for the accommodation of the visitor, are the places that the customers take their meals in.

The first restaurant in the modern sense to be designed for eating as a public activity preceded the *Building News* correspondence by nearly a decade but was obviously still a rarity. Simpson's in the Strand was originally opened as a 'chess divan' in 1828 by a Mr Ries. Twenty years later he was joined by a professional caterer, John Simpson, and the pair rebuilt the premises and reopened them as Simpson's Tavern and Divan. The new restaurant on the ground floor kept the traditional compartments along one wall, but the rest of the space was given over to individual tables in the way that was to become common; the *Builder* on 16 December 1848 commented that 'the general effect of the room is good' and remarked on the 'novel character' of the furniture — 'the round tables being particularly good'.

Enlarged in 1865, the original Simpson's was demolished in 1900 to allow the widening of the Strand, but it was reopened four years later; the main downstairs restaurant preserves the atmosphere of the original with its boxes. The rapid success of Simpson's inspired a whole series of open-layout restaurants, in both purpose-designed and converted buildings, many of them offering a choice of dining rooms. By the end of the century, eating out was becoming a pleasurable experience in its own right, served by an emergent catering industry created by a new breed of entrepreneurs operating chains of restaurants.

LIBRARIES

In the Middle Ages books were rare and valuable acquisitions. They were kept locked in special cupboards or chests — sometimes ornately decorated — to be consulted when required or, if needed more regularly, chained to desks in churches and monasteries; for religious foundations were the birthplace of libraries as they were of schools and hospitals. By the twelfth century monasteries were building special rooms for the storage of books, which the monks would take out into the light of their cloisters to read, and by 1283 these arrangements had been improved by the development of the carrel — a booth with a desk and seat for a single monk, set against a cloister window for natural illumination; in Gloucester Cathedral, a former abbey church, a row of twenty stone carrels can still be seen in the cloister. The best surviving example of a chained library is in Hereford Cathedral, where the original library room was in the late fifteenth-century west cloister (long since demolished).

The oldest surviving library building in Britain is the room above the Congregation House of the Church of St Mary the Virgin, in Oxford. This is the parish church of Oxford and the place where all university ceremonies were staged until the completion in 1669 of the Sheldonian Theatre, designed by Sir Christopher Wren. The library room was built in about 1320 by Bishop Cobham of Worcester, to house the collection of books which he presented to the university. The library remained at St Mary's until 1490 when it was transferred into the newly completed Duke Humphrey's library, the earliest part of the university's Bodleian library, which now has the second greatest collection of books in the UK after the British Museum. The original library in St Mary's is now used as a parish room.

The first library to be built as part of the overall plan of a college was that of New College, Oxford, founded in 1379 by William of Wykeham, Bishop of Winchester. The library forms part of the eastern range of Great Quad, completed by 1386. The plan of the college is generally ascribed to Wykeham himself, the founder of Winchester College which opened in 1394 (see page 38, Education buildings). Both were built by William Wynford, a prominent master mason who had earlier been the royal clerk of works at Windsor Castle.

Libraries at this time were small: not only because the number of people who could read was limited, but also because of the sheer laboriousness of copying manuscripts manually, prior to the arrival of printing in the 1470s. A typical college collection held no more than 400 books, and there were only 2,000 in Oxford University's. College libraries survived the Reformation better than their monastic and ecclesiastical counterparts, which suffered wholesale destruction during the dissolution of the monasteries, collegiate churches and religious guilds in the reigns of Henry VIII and Edward VI. But by 1556 even Duke Humphrey's library at Oxford University had been stripped; only in 1602 was it refounded by Sir Thomas Bodley, from whom it takes its name of the Bodleian.

The dissolution could have proved the opportunity to create a royal, or national, collection, the case for which was being argued (unsuccessfully) as early as 1536. Later attempts during the Tudor period also failed and by the beginning of the seventeenth century the remnants of the once great collections had passed into private hands, from which were eventually to emerge the nuclei of the British Museum (see page 96, Museums) and other educational institutions. By then, printing had created a market for a wide variety of literature amongst a reading public anxious to entertain as well as improve itself, and the stage was therefore set for the public library, which itself enjoys a long and distinguished ancestry.

PUBLIC LIBRARIES

The first public library in Britain preceded the invention of printing by half a century. It was founded by the executors of Richard Whittington, three times Lord Mayor of London, and of another wealthy citizen, William Bury, shortly after Whittington's death in 1423. It was a new building specially designed for the purpose and stood next to the south wall of the City Guildhall, which Whittington had helped to build. Stow, in his *Survey of London*, describes it as a 'fair and large library' and it was solidly built, of stone. The books were chained, as they would have been in an ecclesiastical library, and were largely theological in character. Their readership was virtually exclusively confined to the clergy, students and the educated class of the time. The librarian enjoyed the use of a house with a private garden as a perquisite of office, an indication of the importance attached to this innovation. The collection grew and survived until 1549 when the Duke of Somerset, Protector of Edward VI, carried it away in three cartloads, never to be returned. The following year the City Corporation let the building as a clothing warehouse. This first Guildhall library (the present institution of that name was established in 1828) was one of only a handful of public libraries in Britain in the mid-sixteenth century, none of which survived the Reformation intact.

From then until the early eighteenth century the steadily increasing reading public had to rely largely on endowed libraries given by wealthy benefactors; mostly theological in character, they were usually administered by the local clergy. Town libraries, under municipal rather than ecclesiastical control, were rare and the earliest recorded example was in Norwich, established in 1608 in the house of a municipal official. The eighteenth century, however, witnessed two new developments: circulating lending libraries, run commercially by booksellers, and subscription libraries. The earliest circulating library began operating in 1725 in the Edinburgh High Street bookshop of Allan Ramsay who was born in 1686 in the village of Leadhills, high up in the Lowther Hills in Strathclyde.

It was also in this village that twenty-one lead miners employed by the Scots

Mining Company clubbed together in 1741 to form the first reading society or subscription library in Britain to be set up without benefit of ecclesiastical patronage — eight years before the earliest English equivalent, the Liverpool subscription library. A plaque in the Leadhills library claims that it was instituted by Ramsay. William and Dorothy Wordsworth visited Leadhills in 1803 and in her *Recollections of a Tour made in Scotland* the poet's sister notes with some surprise that the stone building which she had taken to be a school was in fact a library. Single-storeyed, it had steps leading up to a little entrance porch, very much in the style of a village school and of the same stone construction as the miners were encouraged to use in building their own cottages. Other independent subscription libraries followed Leadhills, though mostly for the benefit of the middle rather than the working classes. The Leadhills building survived the closure of the mines in the 1930s and formally reopened after restoration in 1972.

FREE PUBLIC LIBRARIES

The concept of universal free library provision had to await the wave of reforming legislation of the second quarter of the nineteenth century. In 1849 a Parliamentary Select Committee on Public Libraries noted that only one major library in Britain was freely accessible to the public. This was Chetham's in Manchester, the earliest free public library in Britain still in occupation of its original buildings — the first floor of the south and west wings of a fifteenth-century collegiate quadrangle built for priests attached to Manchester parish church (now Manchester Cathedral). The college was dissolved in 1547 and went through an uncertain period in the hands of the Stanley family until being sequestered in the Civil War. It was then that Humphrey Chetham, a prosperous Manchester draper with no heirs, opened negotiations to acquire the buildings for a school and a library, negotiations which were only completed after his death in 1653. The library opened in 1655 with 500 books in the dormitories of the original foundation, and has remained there ever since. Under their fine timber roofs the rooms are filled with deep book bays made by a local joiner, Richard Martinscroft, and fitted with wooden gates after books ceased to be chained in the 1740s. Although originally intended for professional users — clergymen and lawyers, for example — the library was in practice open to all readers from shortly after its inception.

Chetham's library, which still operates as a privately funded public library, remained a lonely outpost until the 1850 Public Libraries Act — this allowed local authorities to fund libraries (and museums) out of their rates (local taxes) and became the foundation of the present library system. The first library to open under the provisions of the new Act was in Winchester (1851) closely followed by Manchester (1852). The new Guildhall library in the City of London had opened earlier, in 1828, but was not open to the public at large until 1873. Winchester's library opened its doors on 10 November 1851 — just under three months from when the Act received the Royal Assent — in the governor's house of the former county gaol, in Jewry Street, which was acquired by the City Council following the building of a new prison.

Plate 24 Chetham's Library, Manchester, the earliest public library still occupying its original buildings. *(Chetham's Library, Manchester)*

The county gaol was built in 1805 to the designs of George Moneypenny. It was a handsome, three-storey edifice of five bays, built in yellow brick with stone quoins and window dressings. The central bay, which housed the governor's quarters, had arched windows and a pediment across the entire upper storey to emphasise its importance, so it was a fitting setting for this milestone in the spread of education. Unfortunately the library had to share the building with the Hampshire Museum and it was neither planned for the lending of books nor particularly well located. A contemporary report in the *Hampshire Chronicle* describes it as being 'stowed away in [a] high and remote part of the building' and appearing 'for all the purposes of study to have been studiously made inaccessible'. Not until 1854 did the library lend out books (from a stock of just over 300); later in the nineteenth century it moved to new premises, and its original home is now Habel's furniture store.

Because of the initially restricted nature of Winchester's enterprise, the honour of opening the first public lending library under the Act went to Manchester Corporation. With an initial collection of 5,300 volumes this opened on 2 September 1852 in the Hall of Science at Campfield which had been built in 1840 as a meeting place for the followers of Robert Owen, a socialist thinker and activist and one of the founders of the Co-operative movement. A dignified, two-storeyed stone-built structure in the Italian style it was paid for by public subscription and acquired on the same basis for £1,200 in 1850 by Manchester Corporation, purchased from the dwindling Owenite community. The lending library was on the ground floor, occupying a spacious room 25.3 by 15.5m (83 by 51ft) and 4.9m (16ft) high; the reference library occupied a similar area upstairs. Prince Albert, the Prince Consort, marked the occasion with a gift of books and a message expressing his

> gratification at seeing Manchester taking the lead, as in many other valuable improvements, in giving practical application to that recent but important act of the legislature, which has recognised for the first time the supply of food for the mind as among those necessaries which in this country are so amply and beneficially supplied to the community by rates.

The Campfield building remained in use until 1877 when the weight of books it contained — by then 18,500 — proved too much for the structure and the library moved to the city's old Town Hall in King Street.

The examples set by Winchester and Manchester were followed enthusiastically by local authorities throughout the country and it became a matter of civic pride to provide for the self-education of their citizens. The first substantial purpose-designed library in Britain was the William Brown Library in Liverpool which opened in 1860. The designers were Thomas Allom and the Corporation architect John Weightman, who set out to complement the neighbouring St George's Hall (see page 26, Civic buildings); the library has been rebuilt following wartime damage.

THE BRITISH LIBRARY

Britain's national library began its existence in a basement reading room in Montagu House, Bloomsbury, the original home of the British Museum (see page 96, Museums). The collection expanded steadily and by the time the library moved into the north wing of the new museum there were some 235,000 volumes to house — the largest collection in Britain. By 1852 it was clear that the only solution to this continuing expansion was a new purpose-designed building, and that the ideal site was the museum's internal quadrangle. Sir Anthony Panizzi, the museum's Keeper of Printed Books, decided that the new reading

Plate 25 The circular reading room at the British Museum. *(British Library)*

room should be circular — like the first such library, the Radcliffe Camera at Oxford, designed by James Gibbs and completed in 1749.

The architect who realised the British Museum reading room was Sydney Smirke, the younger brother of Sir Robert Smirke who had designed the museum; building began in 1854. The structure is of cast iron culminating in the dome which is its most striking feature, and in its construction used technology which had been successfully developed in bridges, factories, markets and buildings such as the Coal Exchange and the Crystal Palace. The completed reading room, with shelving for 1.3 million books and a sophisticated central heating system, inspired library design for the next hundred years, with the Library of Congress in Washington DC — completed in 1897 — as the second best-known of the world's circular reading rooms. But it took less than a century for Britain's national library to outgrow its home in the British Museum and overflow into subsidiary buildings: first the newspaper archive at Colindale, North London; then, after 1945, storage at the former Royal Woolwich Arsenal.

The creation in 1973 of the British Library from the British Museum's and other specialist collections highlighted the need for a purpose-designed library building; initial plans to build this facing the British Museum in Bloomsbury foundered in the face of conservationist opposition to the loss of a Georgian residential area, so the government then bought the 5ha (12.5 acre) site of the former Midland Railway goods depot next to St Pancras station. Plans were approved in 1980 and work began two years later. Designed by Professor Colin St John Wilson, the new British Library is a concrete structure but one covered in a variety of claddings and finishes — stone, brick, timber, aluminium, plaster and paint, with sweeping roofs of slate. The internal space is divided into two wings — one for arts and humanities, the other for sciences — linked by galleries over the entrance hall. The original reading room will be vacated by the British Library in 1996, after which it will be refurbished and used by the British Museum as a reference centre for its own printed material.

MARKETS

The market is the oldest organised form of trading. It is one of the three main contributory functions in the establishment and growth of towns (the others being defensibility and communications), and the grant of a market charter — the earliest on record being given to Chesterfield in 1215 — was a significant step in the acquisition of municipal status. The City of London claimed a monopoly over the establishment of markets within a seven-mile radius under a grant from Edward III in 1327, and only finally lost its prerogative in the confusion of the Civil War. Smithfield is recorded as early as the twelfth century as a horse fair and cattle market held on a 'smooth field' just outside the city walls near the site of St Bartholomew's (see page 73, Hospitals); and the borough's fruit and vegetable market in Southwark, south London, was trading before 1276.

Markets were originally held in the open air, usually in the main streets or squares of towns. In a port city such as London they could also have been on or near the wharves where goods or produce were landed — by the eleventh century Queenhithe and Billingsgate (later the city's main fish market) were established and busy centres of riverborne trade. In large towns, certain streets eventually became identified as the site of specific markets, their rôle still commemorated in names such as Poultry and Cornhill in London. In time, as trade grew and towns prospered, open-air markets tended to become a nuisance because of the congestion they caused in the streets and the resulting obstruction to traffic, and the response of civic authorities — from as early as the thirteenth century — was to put up special buildings to accommodate them; most markets in Britain, however, remained open-air until the nineteenth century and some street markets survive today.

One of the best-known examples is the Sunday market at Petticoat Lane (Middlesex Street) on the eastern boundary of the City of London. Early market buildings in towns throughout Britain were very modest, typically of two storeys with a room for a council chamber or meeting place above, which provided a covered space below for the market which was usually open at the sides. A good example survives in the Old Market House at Shrewsbury, built in 1596.

The earliest fully recorded market building in Britain was the Stocks Market in the City of London, built in the late thirteenth century under a charter of Edward I to rehouse the butchers and fishmongers who had previously sold their wares in the open in Cheapside ('cheap' means market in Anglo-Saxon), one of the oldest streets of the city. The then mayor, Henry de Waleys, wanted them moved from their traditional site in preparation for a royal visit to the city in 1274 'lest any filth should remain in Cheap against the coming of the king'.

He found them a new site, a little further east, on a patch of open ground donated by the Crown at Woolchurchhaw, next to the church of St Mary, Woolchurch. Later, in 1283, he provided the traders with permanent accommodation in the form of a covered market called the Hales (or Stocks) with stalls for letting out to individual butchers or fishmongers — the rents they paid went towards the maintenance of London Bridge.

The Stocks was rebuilt several times, and by the early seventeenth century it was being described as a great 'stone house' divided into separate areas for meat and fish. It was destroyed in the Great Fire of 1666, which also severely damaged St Mary's, and was rebuilt on the site of the church. The new building was described by the contemporary historian John Strype as 'surpassing all other markets in London'. In 1737 it was demolished to make way for the construction of the Mansion House as the official residence of the Lord Mayor of London and the market moved again. Renamed the Fleet Market, its next home was designed by George Dance Senior and situated on a new bridge built over the Fleet River, a tributary of the Thames running under the present-day Farringdon Street; it took the form of two rows of single-storey shops connected by a covered walkway fitted with skylights. In 1826 the site was cleared yet again to allow the building of Farringdon Street which was completed in 1830.

Early markets did not always differentiate as between wholesaling and retailing; both were carried on on the same site, although often at specified times for each kind of trade, and the distinction only began to be formalised in the nineteenth century. By that time a series of purpose-designed market halls was emerging, sometimes on historic sites which had been used as markets for centuries, but planned and built to provision the growing population of Victorian cities. In London, with its plentiful shops and traditional street markets, the new buildings were predominantly wholesale; outside the capital they were mostly retail. The first major covered market hall in Britain was St John's in Liverpool; this was completed in 1822 to the design of the city's architect John Foster and funded by the city corporation at a cost of £35,000.

This 'stupendous building', to quote a contemporary account, was built of brick with stone entrances and details, and covered an area of 6,885sq m (74,115sq ft). The interior was lit by two tiers of windows, and was lined by some sixty shops surrounding a central area which was filled with over 600 market stalls, tables and benches. The contemporary account gives a graphic description:

> On entering the interior, the spectator is amazed at the immense size of the structure, its loftiness, lightness and airiness. It is one large, well-formed and lightly-painted Hall; compared with which, the celebrated Fleet Market is a miserable shed, and Westminster Hall is a moderate-sized room. The whole floor is substantially flagged, and every person resorting to the Market may walk, dry-footed, in every part of the building, alike protected from the cold and rain of the tempest, or the oppressive heat and glare of a summer sun.

The market building was demolished in 1964 and replaced by the St John's shopping centre.

Plate 26 Covent Garden market, alive with customers after its transformation into Britain's first speciality shopping centre. *(Guardian Royal Exchange Assurance Group)*

The oldest survivor of these great nineteenth-century market buildings is at Covent Garden, the one-time convent garden of Westminster Abbey which had long sold its produce to Londoners, and which had been acquired by the Bedford family in the Reformation. Covent Garden market was in existence by 1649 and began as a row of stalls against the south wall of the piazza laid out in 1637 by Inigo Jones for the Earl of Bedford in the centre of his estate. The wall separated the garden of Bedford House, off the Strand, from the piazza — an open space flanked by St Paul's Church to the west and by terraces of town houses which were let to the well-to-do. It was an innovation in British town planning and estate development. Covent Garden secured a royal charter in 1670 as a fruit, flower and vegetable market, and in 1678 its lessees from the Bedford estate built the traders a row of shops against the garden wall. Between 1705 and 1707 Bedford House and its garden were pulled down for the building of Southampton and Tavistock Streets and the market moved closer to the centre of the piazza, in a new row of forty-eight timber booths. A further rebuilding in 1748 created 160 more substantial shops in two rows with cellars.

By the early nineteenth century the Bedford estate was finding it difficult to regulate the traders — especially given the increased demand for space following the closure of the Fleet — and obtained an Act of Parliament to enable it to redevelop the site with an enclosed market building which could be properly controlled and supervised. The architect chosen was Charles Fowler who was working on plans to replace Hungerford market at Charing Cross, a less successful rival to Covent Garden which finally disappeared in 1860 when Charing Cross station was built. Fowler's design provided four parallel ranges of shops which were largely — and in time exclusively — for wholesale use. Construction was basically of brick, with classical stone finishes and colonnades of granite to withstand the knocks of market carts and the first (north) range was completed in 1829. The outer courts between the ranges, originally open to the sky, were covered in by glazed cast-iron roofs in 1875 and 1888. The original market was later extended by additional buildings — the Floral Hall (1860), the Flower Market (1870–1), and the Jubilee Market (1904).

In 1962, after over three centuries of private ownership, the market was acquired under an Act of Parliament by the Covent Garden market authority which began a determined search for a new site — the Ministry of Food had declared the existing one as being 'altogether inadequate' as early as 1921, and the question of moving had remained under consideration for forty years as the congestion caused by motor traffic made efficient operation increasingly difficult. The site finally chosen was Nine Elms, on the south bank of the Thames, where the New Covent Garden Market opened in 1974.

The historic site north of the Strand was initially intended by the Greater London Council for wholesale redevelopment, but pressure from local residents and traders forced a public inquiry in 1971, and two years later the Government listed 245 buildings in the area as being of architectural and historic interest, so ensuring the preservation not only of the central market buildings but of the streets around them. The Fowler building reopened in 1980 as Britain's first speciality shopping centre on the American pattern, as exemplified by the Faneuil Hall in Boston, Massachusetts — both roughly contemporary in their original construction and recent conversion. A speciality centre is characterised by its proponderance of individual traders selling quality goods, it has a good choice of eating and drinking places, with no large department stores, in a setting of architectural and tourist interest.

The converted Covent Garden market has 4,830sq m (52,000sq ft) of trading areas on three levels — the original vaults have been opened up into courtyards with some fifty individual traders. The result is a landmark in the movement for conservation of worthwhile buildings, which initially arose as a reaction to the 1950s and 1960s emphasis on redevelopment.

MUSEUMS

For the Elizabethan philosopher Francis Bacon, writing in *Gesta Grayorum* (published in 1594), there were four requirements for the enjoyment of wisdom. Three of them were a library, a garden and a laboratory; the fourth was a

> goodly huge cabinet, wherein whatsoever the hand of man by exquisite art or engine hath made rare in stuff, form or motion; whatsoever singularity, chance and the shuffle of things hath produced; whatsoever Nature has wrought in things that want life and may be kept, shall be sorted and included.

Bacon's cabinet (ie room) is the direct ancestor of the modern museum. Collecting was very much in the spirit of his age; to quote Impey and MacGregor in *The Origins of Museums* (see page 184, Bibliography): 'interest in the natural world was a major preoccupation of Renaissance learning, and here collecting was to play an indispensable role.' The church, universities and royalty were important collectors of 'treasures' — as early as the twelfth century, Bishop Henry of Winchester brought back a haul of antiquities from a visit to Rome, and the Bodleian library at Oxford University had a gallery devoted to rarities from the year of its foundation in 1602. Henry VIII appointed John Leland as King's Antiquary to list antiquarian material in England and Wales; and Charles I built up a considerable art collection in Whitehall Palace. Most collections remained private, although in 1670 the Royal Armouries in the Tower of London were opened to the public.

The century following Bacon's prescription saw the emergence of a new breed of private collectors. The most important were the antiquary William Camden; Sir Robert Cotton, who travelled in company with Camden and whose legacy ultimately became one of the foundations of the British Museum and of the British Library; and the naturalist dynasty of the John Tradescants, the younger of whom was Charles I's royal gardener. The Tradescants took advantage of their royal and aristocratic patronage, and of their botanical visits abroad, to widen their interests and displayed the results in their house at Lambeth, south London. Their Ark of Novelties constituted the first public collection in Britain, and by 1634 amounted to a substantial, if heterogeneous, assembly of items, in the wide-ranging tradition of the cabinet of curiosities (exhibits included a dodo, and what were claimed to be the feathers of a phoenix and the claw of a roc). The collection was divided into two major sections, natural and artificial.

The Ark was eventually inherited by deed of gift by Elias Ashmole, an antiquarian and collector in his own right, who added his own accumulations of rarities, books and coins. In 1677 Ashmole donated the augmented collection

Plate 27 The north front of the Old Ashmolean Museum at Oxford in 1760, from the second edition of Edward Lhuyd's *Lithophylacii Britannici Ichnographia. (Museum of the History of Science, Oxford University)*

to his old university, Oxford, on condition that it was properly housed. The university accordingly took upon itself the responsibility of providing a building which would house both the collection as well as a school of natural history and chemistry. The result was the Old Ashmolean Museum in Broad Street, Oxford which was completed in 1683 and officially opened by the future James II. The architectural historian Dr J. Mordaunt Crook describes it as 'the first great museological institute specifically designed for exhibition purposes, open to the public and organised on a pedagogical basis'.

It was very much a practical institution with a laboratory in the basement, lecture hall on the principal floor and museum above, each basically a single large room but with the whole composition gaining prominence from the dramatic pedimented portico at its east end. The architect was the Oxfordshire master mason Thomas Wood. The museum was organised for the display of different kinds of exhibits — antiquities, curiosities and natural history specimens — a layout which Dr Cook suggests may have derived from an unexecuted plan by

Wren for new premises for the Royal Society in London. For over 175 years, the Ashmolean served as the university's chief centre for scientific study. In 1845 its non-scientific exhibits moved to the New Ashmolean Museum in Beaumont Street, built to the designs of C. R. Cockerell, to allow more room for the scientific collection. During the latter half of the nineteenth century, however, this was dispersed to a new generation of specialist museums, the most important of them the University Science Museum (completed in 1886) and the ethnographical Pitt Rivers Museum (1886). In 1925 the Old Ashmolean became the university's Museum of the History of Science, a rôle which it continues to fill today.

The original Ashmolean pre-dated by seventy years the foundation of the British Museum, the world's first public national museum. This was created in 1753 by Act of Parliament to provide a permanent home for three great collections — those of Sir Robert Cotton, Sir Hans Sloane and Robert Harley, Earl of Oxford which had at various times been presented to, or purchased by, the state. Wren had in fact been commissioned to design a building for the Cotton Collection of medieval manuscripts after it had finally come into the possession of the state in 1700, but nothing had come of the project. By the mid-eighteenth century the need was urgent if the Cotton archive, the Harleian library of books and manuscripts and, above all, the collections of natural history, art, antiquities, coins and medals assembled by Sir Hans Sloane were to be properly preserved. Sloane's will specified that he wished his collections to 'remain together . . . chiefly in and about the city of London . . . where they may . . . be of most use'.

In 1753, the year of his death, George II gave Royal Assent to the Act creating the British Museum, the funds for the construction of which were to be raised by a public lottery. For reasons of economy the newly appointed museum trustees decided to convert an existing building and the first home of the British Museum was Montagu House, in Bloomsbury, the property of the Earl of Halifax. It was acquired in 1754, converted (possibly by Henry Keene), and opened to the public in 1759. Originally Montagu House had been built in 1675–80 for the first Duke of Montagu, a courtier of Charles II, to the design of Robert Hooke. In brick with stone dressings, it was a town house laid out round a courtyard in the French style; in 1686 it had been gutted by fire, and was then restored internally by a French interior designer.

As a museum, it was divided internally into three departments, each with its own suite of rooms: for manuscripts, medals and coins; books, drawings and maps; and 'natural and artificial productions'. In 1807 this last department was subdivided to create a fourth, of antiquities, and the new Townley Gallery wing opened in 1808 to accommodate it. However, between 1815 and 1825 the museum acquired five major collections, and there was no room to display these properly in Montagu House. When the Elgin Marbles, brought to London by Lord Elgin from the Parthenon in Athens, were purchased by the government in 1816 they had to be unceremoniously installed in a prefabricated shed of timber-frame construction, clad in a skin of single brickwork. In 1821 therefore, the trustees decided to create a purpose-made building and Robert Smirke was given the task of designing it. Smirke had absorbed the classical and neoclassical architecture

Plate 28 The main south front of the British Museum. *(British Museum)*

of Europe on a Grand Tour lasting from 1801 to 1805, and this had determined his career, resulting in his becoming one of the greatest exponents of the Greek Revival — the pure Greek style which he found the noblest of all.

Smirke had set up his own practice by 1807, and in 1815 reached the peak of his profession by being named one of three architects attached to the Office of Works, the state department concerned with royal and government buildings — it acquired responsibility for the British Museum in 1815 and held it until 1960. The chosen site was that of Montagu House, which was to be demolished in stages for the new building. The plan was an elongated quadrangle with the main front, on Great Russell Street, in the form of a classical Greek temple; its colonnade was modelled, according to Dr Crook, on that of the new Dublin Parliament House designed by Sir Edward Lovett Pearce. Work began in 1823 and was completed in 1857, the final stages under the supervision of the architect's younger brother Sydney Smirke since Robert had retired due to ill health in 1846. (The younger Smirke was also the architect of the circular Reading Room — see page 86, Libraries.) In its construction, the museum embodied a great deal of new building technology: concrete foundations; fireproof slate flooring; cast-iron beams, some of them over 15m (50ft) long; and central heating. The walls are of huge slabs of Portland stone fixed to a core of brick. The British Museum is the largest classical building in Britain; but, despite its size, there was concern over the capacity of the galleries even before their completion and this was heightened as the Victorian thirst for knowledge brought streams of new exhibits during the second half of the nineteenth century.

The only substantial extension was opened in 1914, adding the Edward VII Galleries designed by John James Burnet. Long before then, however, the British Museum had adopted the same solution as the Old Ashmolean — namely, dispersal. First to go in 1825 were the paintings (see Art galleries, below); next were the natural history collections which went to the Natural History Museum in South Kensington. Designed in Romanesque Gothic style by Alfred Waterhouse and opened fully to the public in 1886, the Natural History Museum stands in the South Kensington academic precinct, the land for which was purchased out of the proceeds of the 1851 Exhibition (see page 51, Exhibition centres). It was followed by the Victoria and Albert Museum (1909), the Science Museum (1913) and the Geological Museum (1935). Together with the Albert Hall, Imperial Institute, Imperial College and other colleges, they form the earliest planned collection of cultural institutions.

Outside London, Liverpool had a short-lived museum as early as 1800, and in 1821 the Leeds Philosophical Society established a private museum which later opened to the public; but the real surge of local interest followed the 1845 Museums Act which allowed public funding in areas with populations of 10,000 or more. During the nineteenth century the number of public museums rose from fewer than a dozen to over 250, and today there are more than 2,000 (including art galleries), two-thirds of them founded since 1945. For most of their history, museums relied on static displays — exhibits in glass cases with labels; by the 1970s, however, there was a move towards more imaginative and interpretative forms of presentation, using tableaux, reconstructions, themed exhibits and creative design techniques. The first museum which was purpose-designed and built to exploit modern interpretative techniques was the Museum of London, which opened in 1976 after seventeen years in the planning stage. Its architects Powell and Moya had to fit their building into a complicated site at the western end of London Wall in the City. With 3,900sq m (42,000sq ft) of exhibition space, the museum's 330-odd displays (containing over 7,500 individual items) are arranged by period and topic, rather than in specialist galleries of the traditional type.

ART GALLERIES

The art gallery is a specialised form of museum which developed in response to the perception that paintings and sculpture have distinctive qualities — of vivid portrayal and artistic development — which mark them out from other subjects for exhibition. It shares with the museum an ancestry of private collections which came in time into the public domain. Charles I's inherited paintings, which hung in his palaces of Whitehall, Windsor and Hampton Court, would have anticipated developments by two centuries had they passed to the nation; in the event most were sold after his execution, and more were lost when Whitehall Palace burned down in 1698. Among aristocratic collectors, Thomas Howard, Earl of Arundel, had a gallery built in the early seventeenth century at his London mansion, Arundel House, for his collection of Roman sculpture; this was the first of its kind in England, and was eventually presented to Oxford University.

The first independent building put up to exhibit publicly a collection of works of art was the Dulwich Picture Gallery in south London, completed in 1814. The designer was Sir John Soane, architect of the Bank of England and (in 1809) of what was to become the Soane Museum in Holborn — a two-storey gallery behind no 13 Lincoln's Inn Fields, which he subsequently bought and rebuilt as his own house-cum-museum in the Tradescant tradition. He modelled the Dulwich gallery, with its suite of five exhibition rooms, on the Fine Rooms at Somerset House (see page 70, Government buildings). The collection which the gallery housed was originally assembled by an art dealer, Noel Desenfans, and subsequently bequeathed to Dulwich College where, although accessible to the public, it remained a private collection administered by a private trust.

Paintings and statuary formed part of the British Museum's collections, but until well into the nineteenth century, no thought was given to creating a comparable public art gallery of national status as an independent institution. By that time, Britain was lagging behind most other European countries which had built national galleries as symbols of national pride and prosperity. A British equivalent was first mooted in 1799 by Noel Desenfans, six years after part of the Louvre in Paris had opened to the public during the French Revolution; but nothing was done for another quarter century. In 1823 the connoisseur Sir George Beaumont offered to give the nation his collection of old masters if a suitable building were provided. The following year the government found itself sufficiently affluent, thanks to repayment of a foreign loan, to purchase another thirty-eight works which had come onto the market following the death of a wealthy London merchant, John Julius Angerstein. A Treasury Minute dated 23 March 1824 records that:

> His Majesty's Government, having decreed it ... highly expedient that an opportunity which presented itself of purchasing the choice collection of pictures belonging to the late Mr Angerstein should not be lost ... entered into a negotiation with the executors and representatives of that gentleman, and concluded an agreement for the purchase of the whole collection ... for £57,000.

At this time, work was under way on the east wing of the new British Museum, which was originally intended to house the national collection on the first floor. Instead, the embryonic national collection was temporarily displayed in the Angerstein town house at no 100 Pall Mall, while plans went ahead for a purpose-designed national gallery. The site selected was the north side of Trafalgar Square, which was laid out in the early 1830s on the site of the Royal

Mews (stables) as part of the Charing Cross improvement scheme conceived by John Nash. The architect was William Wilkins who claimed to have suggested the gallery as a suitable replacement for the Mews. An energetic exponent of the Greek Revival, he had to work within a long, narrow site — only later did land at the rear become available for a progressive series of extensions; he created a series of top-lit galleries at upper level, flanking an entrance hall and with offices below. His portico is designed as a dramatic setting for the principal entrance which sweeps upwards from the street to the main exhibition level. The National Gallery opened in 1838.

Outside London, the National Gallery of Scotland opened in Edinburgh in 1858, closely following the London model; otherwise, regional and local galleries were slow in coming — perhaps because museums were considered of greater practical value in education. Not until 1877, for example, did Liverpool have its Walker Gallery, and Bristol was even later (1905). The Tate Gallery was built in 1897 on the site of the Millbank Penitentiary (see page 136, Prisons) for the display of British art; it made one of the most recent and imaginative contributions to the artistic resources of the regions when it opened a branch, the Tate Gallery of the North, in Liverpool's Albert Dock (see page 37, Docks).

OFFICES

Originally offices were simply rooms set aside for business in other buildings. These could be royal palaces or noblemen's castles; churches, cathedrals, abbeys or monasteries; warehouses; or the halls of the medieval merchants' and craftsmen's guilds. The livery companies of the City of London, which began as friendly societies gathering in churches or other religious foundations, were from the fourteenth century benefitting from the town mansions which were given to them by wealthy members; the large open-roofed halls which were used for meetings and ceremonies survived as the central feature of later rebuildings and newly built livery halls, and off these were special rooms for the company's funds and records. By the end of the sixteenth century there were forty-eight livery halls, and individual merchants could transact business in their halls or in other communal commercial buildings — from the sixteenth century they had the benefit of the Royal Exchange; from the seventeenth, the coffee houses which opened in towns throughout Britain and soon became business as well as social centres; and in the Victorian era the commodity exchanges (see page 45, Exchanges and financial markets).

But from the earliest times the merchant's principal place of business was in part of his own home, and the tradition of living over the shop or 'counting house' survived well into the nineteenth century. It is preserved in Hoare's Bank in Fleet Street in the City of London, the last of the old-fashioned private deposit banks in the country whose present buildings — the oldest surviving of their kind — date from 1830. The bank was founded in 1672 in Cheapside by Robert Hoare, the son of a Buckinghamshire horse dealer and a member of the craft of goldsmiths who in the seventeenth century began to turn their experience of precious metals into the beginnings of the modern paper-based banking system. In 1690 Hoare decided to move to Fleet Street, which was more convenient for clients living in the newly fashionable West End, and bought from another goldsmith a five-storeyed town mansion called the Golden Hinde where he and his family lived over the banking hall. Here the business flourished and expanded into neighbouring houses.

The tradition of the family town mansion carried over into Hoare's present building which was completed on the same site in 1832 and continues today — if not on a permanent basis. The architect was Charles Parker, an early exponent of the Italianate style which became one of the themes of early Victorian commercial architecture. His Fleet Street elevation is a restrained design in Bath stone, enlivened with sufficient variety in the windows and projecting end bays to add visual interest; with the exception of the later balconies it is unchanged today. The entrance opens into the 'shop' (as the banking hall is called in honour of its origin in a goldsmith's), off which are the former partners' room (now foreign exchange) and counting house (now customer services). All retain their original panelling and, despite modern computer technology in the background, the atmosphere is of nineteenth-century banking with no security screens or grilles separating customers from staff.

Above is the house. The main reception room on the first floor is now the bank's museum and library, while still in use across a corridor are the partners' dining and drawing rooms. The second floor used to serve as quarters for the sleeping-in partner until it was converted to offices; partners staying in town now make use of the attic storey formerly occupied by living-in servants and clerks as a company flat. The twentieth-century demand for increased office accommodation has been met by the addition of new buildings (in 1929 and again in 1956-60) around the bank's rear courtyard — still a remarkably tranquil enclave in the heart of London — and by using the

Plate 29 The 'shop' (banking hall) of Hoare's Bank, Fleet Street. *(C. Hoare and Co)*

cellars of the Mitre Tavern, a favourite of Dr Johnson, on the site of which the bank stands.

Buildings designed specifically and exclusively for office use were rarities until the 1820s. The earliest was the headquarters of the East India Company, completed in 1729 to the scale of (and on the site of) the company's original home in the great City mansion of Sir William Craven at the corner of Leadenhall Street and Lime Street where the Lloyd's building now stands (see page 46, Exchanges and financial markets). The company had received its charter from Queen Elizabeth I, and began as a consortium of merchants with interests in Far Eastern trade, finally becoming the British government's agent in India. The headquarters building was designed by Theodore Jacobsen, a successful trader with Hanseatic connections as well as an architect, and the construction was supervised by John James, a London surveyor who succeeded Sir Christopher Wren as surveyor to the fabric of St Paul's Cathedral. East India House was enlarged in 1799 by Richard Jupp, the company's surveyor for the last thirty years of his life, and finally demolished in 1862, four years after the abolition of the East India Company which followed the suppression of the Indian Mutiny. The British government took over the company's functions, and also the responsibility for governing India — a new India office was provided for in the complex of government offices being built in Whitehall (see page 70, Government buildings).

The original East India House was completed earlier than the first permanent home of the Bank of England. The Bank was formed under an act of 1694 to enable the government to raise money or finance a war against France, and began its existence in the hall of the Mercers' Company, moving shortly after into another livery hall, that of the Grocers in Poultry, where it remained until 1734. Ten years previously the Bank had bought a plot of land in Threadneedle Street — including the house of the first governor, Sir John Houblon — and its first permanent home was designed for this site, in the Palladian style by the Bank's surveyor, George Sampson. The building was later extended and then rebuilt by Sir John Soane, who became the Bank's surveyor in 1788; Soane designed a great cluster of banking halls in the neo-classical style, surrounded by a screen wall — and this is all that survives today of his composition after rebuilding in the 1920s and 1930s. However, in 1988 the Bank re-created, as a museum exhibit, the interior of the bank stock office, the first of Soane's banking halls which had originally been completed in 1792.

Buildings of national significance such as East India House and the Bank of England anticipated by a century the commercial palazzi of the Victorians; however, many of the new private businesses which were emerging occupied comparatively humble premises. By the end of the Georgian era a few houses were being let out as offices, with these occupying separate floors, and an early indication of changes to come was the erection in about 1823 of the first recorded purpose-built block of chambers (or what would now be called speculative offices) at the Lombard Street end of Clements Lane in the City of London. The architect was Annesley Voysey, the grandfather of the better-known domestic architect

Charles Annesley Voysey. Unfortunately, no description or illustration survives of this eventful prototype, but within half a century of its building the faces of cities had changed completely. In 1864 Edward I'Anson could tell the Royal Institute of British Architects, whose president he became in 1886, that: 'there is scarcely a private house left in the City. All are pulled down or converted into offices.' I'Anson also produced an outline specification for these early offices:

> In these buildings, the greatest attention is paid to the size of the rooms, so that the greatest number may be obtained from the smallest space, and that they may be abundantly lighted; convenience of access, the position of doors, stairs, fireplaces and water and gas supply are all carefully noted.

London's experience was soon being repeated in Britain's other commercial centres. Behind this wave of office building lay the explosion of business activity which characterised the Victorian age, fuelled by the Industrial Revolution in which Britain led the world and by her rapid commercial expansion overseas which needed new qualities of managerial expertise to sustain it. Paperwork had previously been minimal and middlemen virtually non-existent, but administration and finance were now becoming distinct functions which demanded specific personnel and accommodation for their efficient performance.

Responding both to the new opportunities and to the need to house their enterprises adequately, Victorian businessmen soon abandoned the tradition of living over the shop and looked for larger and exclusively commercial premises in towns. For their homes they chose the newly fashionable suburban and even rural areas, from which they travelled by the rapidly developing railway and omnibus systems. The original sites of their homes therefore became available for redevelopment as more purpose-designed offices, so creating new commercial enclaves. The invention in 1876 of the telephone (see page 152, Telephony buildings) accelerated the process — offices, factories and warehouses no longer needed to be in close proximity for their owners to run them efficiently, and this precipitated the separation of towns into commercial, industrial and residential districts, which was to be consolidated in planning legislation in the following century.

Banks and insurance companies led the move towards purpose-designed premises, as their directors realised the advertisement value of a prominent and imposing building in attracting business. The County Fire Office in Regent Street, Westminster was the first to be purpose-designed on a new site for a specific commercial client and was completed in 1819 with Robert Abraham as architect. The building formed part of the Quadrant of Regent Street, John Nash's great metropolitan improvement of the West End of London, and was based on the design of the south front of Somerset House, the great government office complex completed in 1800 (see page 70, Government buildings). It was demolished in 1924 for the rebuilding of Regent Street. Two early survivors are the Law Life Assurance at no 187 Fleet Street, designed in the Jacobean style by John Shaw and completed in 1834; and Atlas House in King Street, completed in 1836 by Thomas Hopper in the Italianate style which was to distinguish so many of the new commercial edifices of the Victorian age.

Plate 30 The County Fire Office in Regent Street, from an etching of 1913 by Randolph Schwabe published in *Disappearing London* by E. Beresford Chancellor. *(The Studio, 1927)*

The historical analogies were apt. Given a new building type to design for architects could relevantly look back to the palazzi of the rich merchant classes of the Italian Renaisssance who had provided such valuable patronage for the architectural profession. In fact historical monumentality remained dominant in office design until World War II. Throughout the twentieth century Britain was an architectural as well as a geographical island, largely unaffected by the functional approach and technical innovations of the modern style that became increasingly influential in North America and Europe. And it was not until the 1950s that Britain built a single example of the most dramatic urban innovation of the nineteenth century, the 'skyscraper' or office tower.

OFFICE TOWERS

The structural problems of high-rise development had been solved in the USA by 1885, following the realisation that tall buildings could be hung on internal frames rather than jacked up on loadbearing masonry walls which, apart from the labour of constructing them, occupied valuable space and were subject to physical limits on the height which they could reach. Furthermore, in 1852 Elisha B. Otis had invented the safety passenger lift, and this could now be fully exploited. By the end of the nineteenth century New York and Chicago were vying with each other to erect increasingly tall and imposing buildings; but British cities remained overwhelmingly low-rise, dominated by church spires and town hall towers. A 1956 report by the former London County Council (LCC) noted that 'three-quarters of London's buildings are four storeys or less in height, except for church steeples and architectural features'. Powers to control building heights had first been introduced in 1667 following the Great Fire and were specifically conferred on the LCC in 1890, but they were not often called in aid.

There were three main reasons for this. One was conservatism on the part of commercial developers who, encouraged by local authorities, were assembling previously separate sites for large scale development and filling them up to their

Plate 31 Fountain House, Fenchurch Street, from a drawing produced shortly before its completion in 1957. (*W. H. Rogers*)

perimeter boundaries on the 'jelly mould' principle with squat, low buildings grouped around internal courtyards. These perimeter buildings had to be low — normally a maximum of seven storeys, with the uppermost ones stepped back — to preserve the rights to light of adjacent occupiers. Finally there were the fire regulations — these had kept the 64m (210ft) high tower of the Senate House of London University unoccupied for years after completion in 1937 because it was beyond the reach of firefighting equipment. Only in 1954 was firefighting permitted from within buildings.

What finally brought the skyscraper to Britain was the fact that local authorities revised their policy regarding high buildings, and came to identify them as acceptable landmark features in proposals for large-scale urban redevelopment. By 1956 the LCC was encouraging the inclusion of tall buildings in selected comprehensive development areas; among them was the South Bank, the site of the 1951 Festival of Britain, where its plans included a visual landmark — 'an office building of over 300ft (91m), carefully sited as a vertical feature in a group of public and semi-public buildings' — which became reality as the 1963 Shell Centre. But the first commercial office tower to depart completely from previous practice was Fountain House in Fenchurch Street, City of London, a 1957 development by the City of London Real Property Co Ltd. It was designed by W. H. Rogers, of the company's architectural department, with Sir Howard Robertson (later the designer of the Shell Centre) as consultant architect, and its fourteen storeys rose 52m (170ft) at the centre of the site, which was covered at street level by a two-storey podium block; the whole scheme contained 9,290sq m (100,000sq ft) of office space.

Edmund Howard was the chairman of City of London Real Property and in 1956 was named one of the *Architects' Journal*'s 'men of the year'; in the 19 January issue of the journal that year he described how the original scheme on a smaller site would have produced a building of 'no particular merit', after rights to light and other restrictions had taken their toll — so he set about enlarging the site to allow scope for something he could be proud of. Howard Robertson brought transatlantic influences to bear on the revised design; American born but of British parents, he had been appointed in 1947 as the UK member of the Board of Design Consultants set up to advise on the United Nations headquarters building in New York which was completed in 1950. The towering administration block, with its sides of glazed curtain walling, proved a lasting influence on the development of high-rise buildings; but Robertson had strong views on the appropriateness of materials and insisted that the Shell Centre, his own landmark, should be clad (like early American skyscrapers) in stone — which he saw as the right finish for a major British building, however tall.

In the generation since the completion of Fountain House and the Shell Centre, the high-rise office tower has become the dominant note of the commercial city centre, built on a structural steel or reinforced concrete frame and typically clad (despite Robertson) in light materials such as glass curtain walling.

PALACES

Until the thirteenth century royal power in Britain was exercised on the move. The Saxon and Norman rulers of England and the Scottish kings travelled with their courts around the country, reinforcing their rule by the most effective available means — that of showing themselves in person to their subjects. The king ruled from wherever he was at the time: a royal palace (of which pre-AD1000 examples have been investigated at Yeavening, Northumbria and Cheddar, Wessex), an abbey or the house or castle of the lord who was entertaining him. The concept of a national capital, where the functions of kingship and government were exercised on at least a semi-permanent basis, did not exist before the tenth century in England and the eleventh in Scotland, when the two nations respectively became unified kingdoms.

By 927 Athelstan, of the royal dynasty of the southern Saxon kingdom of Wessex, had extended his rule over the whole of England, and Winchester — the most important town of Wessex — acquired one of the most important marks of capital status when the royal treasury found a permanent home in the old royal palace in the city (see page 66, Government buildings). But Winchester's reign was short. Edward the Confessor, who acceded to the throne of England in 1042, preferred Westminster where the Danish king Cnut had built a palace earlier in the eleventh century and, although William the Conqueror rebuilt Winchester palace and held some of his great feudal assemblies there, the future of London as the national capital and principal royal residence was already secure.

The Confessor is shown enthroned in his palace at Westminster in the Bayeux Tapestry, the earliest contemporary illustration of a British royal residence, which depicts a large hall house of two storeys protected by towers. Immediately next door is Edward's new Abbey Church in which he was buried a few days after its consecration in 1066. Westminster was originally a religious site, with an important monastery which was founded — or refounded — in the second half of the tenth century by King Edgar; an eleventh-century monk ascribes the original foundation to a seventh-century Saxon king, but this may owe more to a desire to establish precedence over the City of London and St Paul's than to a concern for strict historical accuracy. Cnut probably took the opportunity to establish a residence here while he was reviving the monastic community and its church after the wars and invasions which preceded his reign.

The site had important advantages for both monarch and monks, since it was on an island (called Thorney, 'the isle of thorns') which was separated from the north bank of the Thames by two arms of the River Tyburn. It was therefore remote enough for monastic seclusion while for the monarch it was conveniently detached from the City of London, whose citizens were notoriously independent-minded; even William the Conqueror took care to secure Westminster as his base before attempting to deal with them. William built a number of new royal dwellings, among them the Tower of London (see page 61, Fortresses), and also one which is the oldest building in Britain and the world to have been in continuous use as a royal home — Windsor Castle.

Erected originally in 1080 as a defensive citadel at an important Thames crossing to the west of London, Windsor Castle was rebuilt in the late twelfth century by Henry II, and again as a residence in the period after 1350 by Edward III, who was born there. His architect, William of Wykeham, built the king a set of royal apartments in the eastern (upper) end of the castle. Ranged at first-floor level over vaulted undercrofts, these form the northern side of a quadrangle, together with a chapel and a hall; an arrangement that Wykeham was to repeat in his New College, Oxford and at Winchester College (see page 38, Education buildings). Subsequent rebuildings in the seventeenth and nineteenth centuries (most comprehensively under George IV) have removed virtually all traces of Wykeham's work, with the exception of the inner gateway leading into the upper ward, and the undercrofts. The quadrangular arrangement, however, survives.

Windsor Castle remains very much in use as one of the Queen's three official residences, the others being Buckingham Palace in London and Holyrood House in Scotland, whose origins are nearly as old as Windsor's. Holyrood, on the outskirts of Edinburgh, was founded in 1128 as an Augustinian abbey by the early twelfth-century Scottish king, David I. His successors took regular advantage of the canons' hospitality and by the fifteenth century Holyrood had become an established royal residence and the setting for important councils of state. It was rebuilt by kings James IV and V as a quadrangular palace in the early years of the sixteenth century; sacked by the English during Henry VIII's 'rough wooing' of Mary Queen of Scots as a bride for the future Edward VI; and after further damage during the Civil War, it was rebuilt again for the restored Charles II. Since his reign the palace has technically been the royal residence in Scotland.

Buckingham Palace is the main official residence of the royal family, and comes at the end of a succession of London state palaces beginning at Westminster, all of which lay within a small area of central London. Westminster remained the principal royal palace for some 500 years — a period which witnessed the end of the feudal system, the emergence of Parliament and the growth of London, with its twin centres of the City and Westminster, into a great and populous city. What changed Westminster from a royal residence to the home of Parliament was a fire in 1512, after which Henry VIII relinquished the site to the twin institutions of law and government (see page 68, Government buildings); it is still known officially, however, as the Palace of Westminster. The king coveted York House, the originally thirteenth-century town house a short distance to the north which Cardinal Wolsey, Archbishop of York, had enlarged into a palatial mansion, and he secured it on the fall of Wolsey in 1529. York House therefore became York Palace which then became Whitehall Palace.

Three years later the king took over a leper hospital lying west of Whitehall; he

fenced in its lands for deer and had the mason John Molton build him a palace —
St James's Palace, which he intended as a retreat from the bustle of court. It was in
the form of a manor house of brick, which had recently become an acceptable alternative to stone in important buildings. St James's Park is the oldest royal park.

Whitehall remained the principal royal palace until well into the reign of James
II, the last king to live there, whose reign ended in 1688. As with Westminster Hall
to the south, it is survived by one of its later buildings, in this case the Banqueting
House which was designed by Inigo Jones, the first British architect to adopt the
Palladian style, and inaugurated in 1622. From the outside, it appears to be on
two storeys but internally it is one great ceremonial space, designed to be used
for theatrical performances (see page 158, Theatres) as well as for state occasions.
Charles I, for whose father it had been built, stepped onto his scaffold through a
window in the Banqueting House after being tried in Westminster Hall. Plans for
rebuilding Whitehall to complement the Banqueting House were being formu-
lated years before the rest of the palace burned down in 1698, but came to nothing.

William III, who followed James II, preferred the drier environment of
Kensington, and he commissioned Sir Christopher Wren to rebuild the Jacobean
Nottingham House as Kensington Palace; but his successor, Anne, designated St
James's as London's official royal palace — which the earlier Stuarts had used for
state occasions and to house their relatives — and spent half of each year there.
St James's still retains its status as the court to which ambassadors to Britain
are credited, although Buckingham Palace has succeeded it as the sovereign's
principal London residence.

The former Buckingham House was built in 1702 by John Sheffield, Duke of
Buckingham. The architect was a Dutchman, Captain Wynne, and it remained
in the Sheffield family until 1762 when George III, who was finding conditions
in St James's cramped and uncomfortable after the birth of his first child, bought
it as a private residence for the royal family away from the formalities of court
life, retaining the older palace for state and ceremonial occasions. However,
it was under his successor, George IV, that the King's House — as it was
by then known — underwent its monumental transformation. The new king's
favourite architect, John Nash, was given the task of remodelling and extending
the building to produce a state palace of the kind in which Britain was finding
herself embarrassingly deficient as compared with other European states. The
rebuilding was still incomplete when George IV died in 1830, and after a government investigation, Nash was dismissed and replaced by Edward Blore; and
he was still at work in 1837, the year of the accession of Queen Victoria who was
the first sovereign to sleep there. Later, to create more space, Blore connected
the two wings of the palace with a new front, so creating an internal courtyard.
The familiar main elevation of Buckingham Palace today dates from 1913 when
it was refaced by Sir Aston Webb; and it was Webb who added the balconies on
which the royal family make appearances on state occasions.

Plate 32 Inigo Jones's Banqueting House, the only survivor of Whitehall Palace. *(Crown
copyright, reproduced with the permission of the Controller of HMSO)*

PARLIAMENT HOUSES

The oldest parliamentary site in the British Isles is Tynwald Hill at St John's, on the Isle of Man. The island is midway between England, Wales, Scotland and Ireland in the Celtic Sea, and has never been part of the United Kingdom; while acknowledging the British sovereign as 'Lord of Mann' and being represented internationally by the UK, it enjoys a tradition of self-government which goes back for more than 1,000 years, to the Viking settlements which began in the ninth century. The invaders brought their Norse tradition of an open-air assembly at which laws were made and promulgated; called the 'Tynwald', from the Norse *Thingvollr* meaning 'field of assembly', they would meet on a mound at the natural crossroads of the island where, in a ceremony held each July, the population still gathers to hear announced, in the Manx and English languages, a summary of the laws passed during the previous twelve months by the Manx Parliament, which now meets in the Victorian island capital of Douglas.

Representative government in mainland Britain has different origins, deriving from the royal councils which attended on the monarch, the Witangemots of the Saxons and the Great Councils of the Normans and Plantagenets. The Great Parliament of 1265 was summoned to meet in London by Simon de Montfort who was the leader of the English barons working to achieve a political settlement with King Henry III, and was the most widespread assembly ever staged, attended not only by lords temporal and spiritual but by knights from each shire and 'burgesses' (citizens) from the chief towns. The venue was Westminster Hall (see page 66, Government buildings) in the king's London palace. Early parliaments met only once or twice a year, but from 1325 the representatives of the 'commons' — the shire and town communities of the country — were always present, and in the early fourteenth century these began to meet separately from the Lords, so initiating the present-day division of the British Parliament (and of those states which have taken Westminster as their model) into two houses.

Since their gatherings were occasional events during the Middle Ages, they made use of rooms in the palace or the nearby Westminster Abbey. A parliamentary session typically began with an opening ceremony in the presence of the king in the Painted Chamber, so-called from its elaborate wall paintings. After the opening ceremony the two houses went their separate ways, the Lords to the White Chamber of the palace (its site now occupied by the Royal Gallery) and the Commons normally to the abbey, where they used the monks' refectory or the chapter house. Completed in 1253 the chapter house was designed on an octagonal plan, large enough to accommodate secular meetings as well as those concerned with the administration of the abbey. The

112

chapter house served as the meeting place of the House of Commons until the reign of Henry VIII.

This monarch had abandoned Westminster after the damage it suffered in the fire of 1512, in favour of Whitehall (see page 109, Palaces), leaving the original royal palace of London available for the use of Parliament which had by now grown into the third great institution of the land, after the Church and the King. In 1547 his successor Edward VI granted the Commons the use of St Stephen's Chapel. This was the king's private palace chapel, begun in 1292 by the mason William of Ramsey for Edward I, who was attempting to emulate in London the Sainte Chapelle in Paris. The Lords had the use of the White Chamber of the palace, while the fourteenth-century Jewel Tower (see page 68, Government buildings) served as parliamentary offices from 1621.

Parliament grew steadily in importance during the late Tudor and Stuart periods, and achieved a permanent role following the 'Glorious Revolution' of 1688 when William III and Mary II supplanted Mary's father, James II. The Declaration of Rights was read in the Banqueting Hall in Whitehall, where the new monarchs were offered the crown; this repudiated the political absolutism which had been sought by the earlier Stuarts, and replaced it with the twin principles of constitutional monarchy and the supremacy of Parliamentary law. The compromise then attained has endured ever since, with the monarch elevated above the clashes of political conflict and Parliament left free to pursue the business of government.

For the next 150 years, however, the Westminster Parliament was obliged to exercise its now acknowledged and increasingly important functions in converted rooms inside a medieval palace. St Stephen's Chapel in particular was a mere 18.3 by 9.15m (60 by 30ft) in area, and had to be progressively enlarged to accommodate increases in the size of the Commons. In 1707, after the union of England and Scotland, Wren carried out major alterations, adding galleries supported on pillars to make room for Scottish members; and James Wyatt was responsible for further work following the 1800 Act of Union which brought more than 100 new Irish members into the Commons. Wyatt's work, completed in 1801, involved cutting back the medieval walls to provide more seating — this was at the expense of a series of brilliant medieval wallpaintings which were revealed once wooden panelling had been removed; these were recorded for posterity and then destroyed.

This expedient did not prove satisfactory for long, however, and in 1816 Sir John Soane, who had become an attached architect to the Office of Works in the previous year, produced plans for a new House of Lords and House of Commons on either side of St Stephen's Chapel, which was to be restored to religious use for members of both Houses. By the 1830s, the case for improved accommodation was overwhelming and it was only the reluctance of the Treasury to commit the necessary finance which stood in the way; however, on 16 October 1834 the debate was finally overtaken by events in the form of a fire. This originated in the House of Lords where, in a fit of misplaced economy, the furnaces had been stoked against the autumnal weather with cartloads of wooden tally sticks which had formerly been used by the Exchequer in its accounting. The chimney flues overheated and caught fire, and overnight the Palace of Westminster was reduced to a ruin before a crowd who, in the contemporary account of one newly homeless MP, Sir John Hobhouse, 'behaved very well'; only one parliamentary critic had to be arrested for cheering when the flames increased. Westminster Hall was saved, but for the rest there was now no alternative to a new building.

Interestingly enough, both the Scots and the Irish already had their purpose-designed parliament houses while the English were making do with their medieval palace. The Scottish Parliament House in Edinburgh was begun in 1637 and completed in 1640 on the one-time site of the graveyard of the High Kirk of St Giles which had, by the early seventeenth century, become the centre of a group of buildings used by the Scottish Parliament or Courts. The architect was Sir James Murray, who was the appointed Overseer of the King's Works in Scotland. The building was of two storeys, and the Parliament Hall, in which the Scottish Parliament sat in a single chamber until its union with the English Parliament in 1707, was on the upper one. It is 36.5m (120ft) long by 12m (40ft) wide and distinguished by a fine hammerbeam roof which was made by John Scott. The Hall survives as an assembly hall for the Supreme Courts of Scotland.

The Irish Parliament House, in Dublin's College Green, was begun in 1728 and the Irish Parliament met there for the first time in 1731. The architect was Captain Sir Edward Lovett Pearce who became the official Surveyor of Works and Fortifications in Ireland in 1730; according to the architectural historian Dr J. Mordaunt Crook, his design inspired that of the British Museum (see page 97, Museums). The building was reconstructed after a fire in 1792 by Vincenzo Waldré, and was then substantially altered in 1802–6 during its conversion into offices for the Bank of Ireland — this followed the 1800 Act of Union which established a single parliament for the whole of the United Kingdom. It still serves as the headquarters of the bank. It is among the ironies of British history that the early purpose-built parliament houses of Scotland and of Ireland survive, although long since divested of their original purpose, while the Mother of Parliaments itself inhabits buildings a mere century and a half old.

After the fire which destroyed the Palace of Westminster the dispossessed parliamentarians were sheltered in temporary accommodation arranged by Sir Robert Smirke, who had earlier performed a similar office for the Elgin Marbles (see page 96, Museums). In the meantime the government announced an architectural competition for the design of new Houses of Parliament; they were to be in the Gothic or Elizabethan style, to the exclusion of the classical or Italian which would previously have been *de rigueur* for a secular building of such importance and scale. Out of ninety-seven entries the winner was Sir Charles Barry, a designer both of Gothic churches and of mansions

Plate 33 The Scottish Parliament House, Edinburgh, older than the present Houses of Parliament at Westminster. *(Joe Rock)*

and clubs in the style of Italian palazzi, who was aided by Augustus Welby Pugin. Their collaboration produced a sublime essay in perpendicular Gothic which set the tone for the design of public buildings for the Victorian era.

Barry's plan has brought order where previously there had been a rambling collection of older buildings. It centres on a spine running north–south along which are ranged all the principal rooms, including the new House of Lords and House of Commons. These are symmetrically ranged on opposite sides of the central lobby where constituents meet their MPs. As a composition the new Houses of Parliament created a wholly appropriate setting for the medieval Westminster Hall and successfully complemented Westminster Abbey, where the Henry VII Chapel was one of the influences on which Barry and Pugin drew. The foundation stone of the new buildings was laid in 1840, the House of Lords was in use by 1847 and the Commons by 1850. Later came the two towers which provide a vertical emphasis at either end, the Victoria Tower over the Sovereign's Entrance and the Clock Tower (the home of Big Ben, Britain's most famous public clock) overlooking Westminster Bridge.

The House of Commons was destroyed by aerial bombing in May 1941 and the present chamber, which opened in 1950, is the work of Sir Giles Gilbert Scott, who produced a simplified version of Barry's original. The Houses of Parliament form part of a precinct which now extends north of Bridge Street as the government has acquired and converted buildings to create offices for MPs and their staffs; the historic palace site has proved increasingly unable to provide sufficient office space to cope with the twentieth-century growth in parliamentary business.

PLACES OF WORSHIP

Given that their function was at least partly religious, the earliest surviving structures erected for worship are the great stone circles which appear on sites throughout Britain from Cornwall to the north of Scotland and the Scottish islands. Avebury in Wiltshire is dated as far back as 3500BC; it is built of boulders of sarsen sandstone from the nearby Marlborough Downs, arranged in a pattern of rings, the outermost of them encircling the part of the present-day village of Avebury which dates from the Anglo-Saxon period. In the eighteenth century a number of the ring stones were removed and broken up as material for buildings in the village. The four roads leading out of Avebury and intersecting the main ring follow the line of ancient avenues of stones which approached the circle from the four cardinal points of the compass. To the extent that Avebury and the other circles also had an astronomical rôle — including Stonehenge which lay 28km (17.5 miles) to the south and Callanish on the Hebridean island of Lewis — this would also give them a claim to be considered as the earliest scientific buildings in Britain. The distinction would not have been relevant to their builders, for whom establishing a calendar was of prime significance for both religion and agriculture which were closely linked in the rhythm of the year.

The earliest religious buildings (as opposed to structures) of which we have archaeological evidence are the temples which the Romans built during their four centuries of occupation from AD43. A temple to Mithras, a god of Persian origin, was discovered in the City of London in 1954 during the redevelopment of a bomb-damaged area in Queen Victoria Street as the Bucklersbury House office complex. The ruins of the temple, built in the second century AD and later converted to a Christian church, have been reassembled outside the complex.

By the early part of the second century Britain came under the influence of Christianity, which in AD313 was to become the official religion of the Roman Empire under the convert Emperor Constantine and spread rapidly in the homeland of his mother, St Helena. A church may have existed in Westminster in the second century AD on the site of the present-day Westminster Abbey and there were churches at important Roman centres such as Lincoln, Silchester (Hampshire), and Canterbury (Kent) — see below. The oldest Christian church so far excavated is at Colchester, Essex. Built — or possibly converted from an earlier pagan temple — around 320, with a later apse added at its eastern end, the church measures 23 by 7.3m (75 by 24ft) and some of its walls have survived to a height of 0.6m (2ft).

The political break with Rome was followed by a century and a half of war between the Romano-British defenders and Germanic invaders from across the

Channel, and affected the development of Christianity in mainland Britain; the faith never completely died out, however, especially in the Celtic areas of the west and north where the monastic tradition was strong and Ireland — evangelised in the fifth century by St Patrick, the son of a Roman British official — was at a close distance. The earliest evidence of this continuing tradition is the stone church which St Ninian is credited with having built on a rocky outcrop at Whithorn in Galloway, south-west Scotland, following his return from Rome in the fifth century AD. Called the *candida casa* (white house) from its external masonry and internal white plastering, its ruined walls stand close to the revived twelfth-century priory cathedral built by Fergus, Lord of Galloway, and the present-day parish kirk of Whithorn — collectively forming a site which has been in use for Christian worship for nearly 1,600 years. Whithorn therefore precedes the better-known Iona in the chronology of British church buildings. Around 563 St Columba arrived from Ireland on this west-coast Scottish island off Mull and established a monastic centre for the evangelisation of Scotland. However, his timber monastery was repeatedly destroyed by Danish raiders and the monks eventually dispersed to Dunkeld, north of Perth in the eastern Scottish mainland, and this became the focus of Christianity in Scotland until the tenth century. The existing monastic buildings on Iona are of thirteenth-century origin on a new site.

The oldest surviving buildings in Britain which have been continuously in

Plate 34 St Martin's Church, Canterbury, Britain's oldest continuously used church from a drawing published in 1813 in *The Gentleman's Magazine*. (*From the collection of Canon Reginald Humphriss*)

use for Christian worship are in Canterbury, Kent. It was here, in 597, that St Augustine began his mission from Rome to re-establish Christianity in the southern part of Britain by converting the heathen Anglo-Saxons. The two waves of missionary activity met eventually in Northumbria, the most northerly area of England on the border with Scotland. The nearest part of Britain to Europe, and so the most susceptible to continental influences, was the Saxon kingdom of Kent which was already in a state of advanced civilisation. Its capital, Canterbury, was built within the walls of the Roman town of Durovernum at a strategic point where the road from the coast to London crossed the River Stour. King Ethelbert of Kent had a Christian wife, Bertha, who was the daughter of the Frankish king of Paris and brought both her personal chaplain Liudhard and her religion when she came to Britain in the 560s or (more probably) 570s.

According to the Anglo-Saxon scholar Bede in his eighth-century *History of the English Church*: 'there stood on the east side of the city an ancient church built and dedicated in honour of St Martin during the Roman occupation of Britain, where the Christian Queen ... came to pray.' Scholars identify the church of St Martin which stands today, 0.5km (0.3 miles) east of the city wall, as Queen Bertha's church. Its oldest part, the western end of the chancel, is built largely of Roman bricks and mortar and uses late Roman building techniques characteristic of the third and fourth centuries AD; the nave is later and was probably built by Augustine's monks re-using Roman bricks mixed with local sandstone (Roman buildings were used as quarries of re-useable material until the eighteenth century).

St Augustine's Abbey and the first cathedral at Canterbury also date from the time of St Augustine; the origin of the cathedral has again been traced back to the Roman period. Enlarged more than once by Anglo-Saxon archbishops it was destroyed by fire in 1067; but the monk Eadmer who had been present as a child at the conflagration compared it with Old St Peter's in Rome. From Eadmer's description, the nave was flanked by aisles with external twin towers and the chancel centred on a great stone altar set in a raised sanctuary. This ancient shrine was replaced by the Norman cathedral built by Lanfranc, who became archbishop of Canterbury in 1070 and, according to contemporary accounts, had largely completed the construction work by 1077.

None of the pre-Norman cathedrals has survived and only ruins (as at Elmham, Norfolk) or fragments incorporated in later work (as at Sherborne, Dorset) remain to bear witness to the comprehensive diocesan structure built up before the Conquest. The Normans created new dioceses which were based on major towns instead of the often rural centres adopted by their predecessors, and they built monuments in stone which like their castles (see page 61, Fortresses), were designed to embody the power and permanence of the new régime. They rebuilt Edward the Confessor's abbey and church at Westminster — but nothing remains of the earlier structure. Parish churches on the other hand, being less important, fared better and reports of new archaeological work carried out in 1988 suggest that as many as 500 churches in England — nearly double the previously estimated total of 270 — are of Anglo-Saxon origin.

Plate 35 The interior of St Etheldreda's Church, Holborn, the oldest church in Britain used for Roman Catholic worship. *(Photograph by Marc Henrie, reproduced by kind permission of the rector)*

CATHOLIC CHURCHES

In the Reformation, all existing places of Christian worship came under the control of the new national churches which owed no allegiance to the Pope. For those who remained loyal to Rome, penal legislation meant practising their religion in secret. The Catholic Relief Acts of 1778 in England and Ireland and 1793 in Scotland were passed when the Hanoverian dynasty was firmly established, and only then were clergy finally free to preach and teach the Catholic faith without fear of prosecution; while in 1791 a further Act legalised church-building and the public celebration of the Mass. Until then the Catholic community had used rooms in private houses, outbuildings and barns and (in London) the embassy chapels of the Catholic European powers and the royal chapels of the Stuart dynasty.

The earliest church to have been purpose-built for Catholic worship after the Reformation is the Queen's Chapel in Marlborough Gate, near St James's Palace, designed by Inigo Jones for the Catholic consort of the future Charles I. Completed in 1625, this was the first place of worship in Britain in an uncompromisingly classical style; it is now a Church of England place of worship. The oldest church building in regular use as a Catholic place of worship is St Etheldreda's in Ely Place, Holborn. Built in about 1290 as the town chapel of the bishops of Ely, it is on two storeys, with the church itself — notable for a fine roof of chestnut timber and the tracery of its east and west windows — standing above an earlier undercroft which incorporates Roman masonry. It was bought near-derelict in 1874 by a religious order, and restored as the first pre-Reformation church in Britain to revert to Catholic worship.

SYNAGOGUES

The oldest synagogue in Britain is that of the Spanish and Portugese Jews' Congregation in Bevis Marks, City of London. Built by Joseph Avis, a Quaker tailor who is reported to have refused to make any profit out of building a House of God, it opened in 1701, forty-five years after the re-establishment of the Jewish community in Britain under the protectorate of Oliver Cromwell. Immigration by Jews began in the reign of William the Conqueror, who recognised their financial skills. By the thirteenth century, however, their position was resented and under threat and in 1290 Edward I decreed their expulsion. No place of worship survives from the days of this original settlement.

By the mid-seventeenth century there was once again a small and unofficial Jewish community made up largely of refugees from persecution in Spain. In 1656, with a guarantee of security from the Lord Protector, the first Jewish place of worship of the resettlement opened in the upper floor of a house in Creechurch Lane, near Aldgate in the City of London. By 1690 the community was thriving and had outgrown its first home, and decided to fund a purpose-built synagogue on a site nearby in Bevis Marks. Fairly undistinguished on the outside, this is arranged internally like a contemporary church as a plain rectangular space with galleries on timber columns, its main feature a magnificent timber Ark of the Covenant for storing the scrolls of the law. Oak benches from the Creechurch

Lane synagogue are built into the seating. Apart from the introduction of electric lighting and radiators, the building is virtually unchanged and remains in regular use for worship.

MOSQUES

The earliest mosque built in Britain is the Shah Jehan in Woking, Surrey. It was completed in 1890 by W. I. Chambers for Dr Gottlieb Leitner who had converted the existing buildings of the Royal Dramatic College, built in 1865, into an oriental study centre which became the first formal focus of Muslim life in Britain. The Mosque is square in plan, under a dome, and set back behind a courtyard. The mihrab, the niche in the main interior wall indicating the direction of Mecca, to which Muslims pray, is precisely aligned; according to a contemporary report in *Building News*: 'a captain of a P&O boat kindly went to Woking and took the bearings.' There are currently some 400 mosques in Britain of which the largest and best known is the Regent's Park mosque, the main Muslim centre in Britain since its completion in 1978 on a site purchased with aid from the British government. The architect was Sir Frederick Gibberd.

POST OFFICES

The Royal Mail was, in origin, precisely that — the means by which sovereigns and their courts sent and received communications by royal messengers. Major roads from London or other important towns were lined with staging posts — usually inns — under the charge of postmasters, whose responsibility it was to see the mail on its way to the next stage and to provide changes of horses for the couriers. Private use of the post was not encouraged until 1635 when Charles I opened the system to the general public, who could use the inns along the way to deliver and collect their mail. Early London posthouses were located in convenient inns; London's 'general post office' was originally the Windmill in Old Jewry and ultimately, the Black Swan in Bishopsgate, dealing with mail from branch offices as well as to and from the provinces.

During the Great Fire of London in 1666, the GPO — only recently re-established after the interregnum of Cromwell's Commonwealth — moved to Covent Garden. In 1678 it moved again to the Lombard Street mansion built by Sir Robert Viner, a banker and former Lord Mayor of London, where it grew steadily under the pressure of business, eventually occupying the entire site bounded by Sherborne Lane and Abchurch Street. A plaque on a building on the corner of Post Office Court and King William Street (which was laid out in the 1830s) records the Post Office's 150 year presence. Not until 1829 did the GPO have its first purpose-built headquarters and by then the postal system had developed dramatically, thanks to the establishment in 1784 of the mail coach system.

The idea came from John Palmer, a Westcountry theatre manager born in Bath in 1742 who faced the problem of moving actors and props between his two theatres, in Bath and Bristol (see page 160, Theatres). He solved it by organising a service of specially built coaches (soon christened 'caterpillars' because of their length) and then realised that the speed, and, even more important, the security of the mails would benefit from similar treatment, with coaches rather than mounted postboys using the much-improved roads that were now being maintained by turnpike trusts. He took the idea to London and gained the support of William Pitt, then Chancellor of the Exchequer, whose interest lay in the fact that the mails were the main means of moving money around the country. The first mail coach ran on 2 August 1784 from the Rummer Inn in Bristol, travelling via Bath and arriving sixteen hours later, on schedule, at the Swan with Two Necks in Lad Lane (later Gresham Street) in the City. Its success brought government endorsement and by 1786 regular mail coaches were running to Dover, Portsmouth, Exeter, Holyhead, Carlisle, Edinburgh and other major towns.

The Swan with Two Necks became London's most important coaching inn, with fourteen mail coaches leaving every night. It was a galleried building extending round a large central courtyard, and together with its booking office and waiting rooms it may have provided the inspiration for Charles Dickens' description of the arrival of Tom Pinch in *Martin Chuzzlewit* (first published in 1843). The inn flourished until the arrival in 1837 of the London to Birmingham Railway, and then its far-sighted proprietor, William Chaplin, went into partnership with Benjamin Horne, of the equally famous Golden Cross at Charing Cross, to found the firm of Chaplin and Horne, and secured the appointment as the railway's parcels and carriage agent. Their inns became booking offices (the ancestors of modern travel agents) and their coaches then ran to provide connections with railway services. The old buildings were eventually pulled down and replaced — the new Swan, built in the 1850s, was listed as a railway agency until well into the twentieth century. At the other end of this pioneering run, the Rummer Inn still stands in St Nicholas' Market, off Bristol High Street. Rebuilt by John Wood on the site of the city's oldest inn, the Green Lattice, its Georgian elevations can be seen from inside the market arcades. (The High Street front is much later and gives no idea of what lies behind.)

During their heyday (the last coach ran in Britain in 1874), the mail coaches brought regular postal communication to towns and villages which had previously been miles away from the nearest main roads. To serve their new customers, hundreds of local post offices were needed, and these were typically in a room in a private house, in the vicarage or village school or (as with sub-post offices today) in a shop — wherever the postmaster's home or business was located. The main requirement, and the post office's distinguishing mark, was a window through which post could be handed in or collected and paid for — until 1840 and the introduction by the postmaster-general, Rowland Hill, of the universal penny-post and prepayment with postage stamps, it was the recipient rather than the sender who paid; while guaranteed home delivery did not become general until 1897.

The oldest post office in the country is at Sanquhar in Dumfries and Galloway, south-west Scotland, which has been in continuous use since 1800 if not earlier. The title deeds of the premises, a small, two-storeyed terraced house, date from 1760, and the town is known to have enjoyed a regular postal service by 1763. Meanwhile, it was increasingly realised that postal services were needed within, as well as between, major towns and cities. A local London service, started in 1680 as a private-enterprise venture, was taken over by the government and incorporated into the national service; while an act of 1765 allowed the establishment of local posts in other towns, a number of which were operational by the end of the century. To administer this growing network of services efficiently, the Post Office eventually needed a properly planned and purpose-designed building.

Its new headquarters, which opened in 1829, stood on the site formerly occupied by the ancient church of St Martin's-le-Grand, and of more than 130 houses which were demolished to clear the necessary two acres of land bounded by St Martin's-le-Grand, Gresham Street, Foster Lane and Newgate

Plate 36 The oldest post office in Britain at Sanquhar, in south-west Scotland. *(Post Office archives)*

Street/Cheapside. Designed by Sir Robert Smirke, the architect of the British Museum (see page 96, Museums), it was built at the joint expense of the State and the City of London, of brick faced with Portland stone. Measuring 116m (380ft) long by 36.5m (120ft) deep, the new GPO was an impressive exercise in the Greek Ionic style; its great central portico of six columns was modelled on the Temple of Minerva at Priene and echoed by four-column variants fronting the north and south wings. It soon became one of the sights of London, with crowds gathering every evening to watch the mail coaches leave from the front entrance for destinations throughout Britain; the novelist Anthony Trollope, in his early days as a post office clerk, gave the Queen of Saxony a guided tour.

Like its predecessor in Lombard Street, the GPO was both a public post office and the headquarters of the Post Office administration. Additional traffic resulting from the introduction of the penny-post in 1840 and the development of new services brought the requirement for extra accommodation, and further storeys were added until the need for new buildings became inescapable. 'GPO West' was completed in 1874 opposite the original premises and in a similar style, and became the home of the GPO's newly nationalised and fast expanding telegraph service the following year; it was from the roof of this building that

Marconi made the first public demonstration of radio in 1896. 'GPO North' was the next headquarters, completed in 1895 on the site of the Bull and Mouth, north of Angel Street and London's second busiest coaching inn after The Swan with Two Necks; and finally the King Edward Building (completed in 1910 on the west side of King Edward Street) provided badly needed additional offices. The original building, 'GPO East', was demolished in 1912. In 1985, the Post Office sold 'GPO North' and moved to the West End of London. 'GPO West' was demolished in 1967 and its site is now occupied by the headquarters of British Telecom, an organisation separate from the Post Office since 1981.

'King Edward' is therefore the only survivor of the original group of buildings still in Post Office ownership. Designed by Sir Henry Tanner, the chief government architect of his day, it is one of the earliest official buildings to have been built in Britain, using reinforced concrete construction, although this is concealed behind a façade of Portland stone on granite plinths to comply with the prevailing architectural standards of the day. Even so, Sir Henry succeeded in gaining some 4,650sq m (50,000sq ft) of office space by being able to reduce the thickness of the external walls. As well as providing an operational post office — once the largest in the country — 'King Edward' is now the home of the National Postal Museum. Erected in 1881 outside its front entrance is a statue of Rowland Hill by Onslow Ford.

Plate 37 The 'King Edward Building' in King Edward Street is the only remaining operational post office building of the original complex which expanded from St Martin's-Le-Grand, seen here from the rear of the former Post Office headquarters. It remains a functioning post office (unusually opulent in décor), and houses the National Postal Museum. *(The Post Office)*

POWER STATIONS

In 1831 Michael Faraday discovered the principle of electromagnetic induction which made possible the mechanical generation of electricity. However, harnessing Faraday's breakthrough to the social and commercial needs of the community took several decades, and the crucial practical development only came in 1867 when William Siemens perfected a generator using self-energising electromagnets to produce steady supplies of power. This technology remains in essence that of a modern power station — unless hydroelectric energy is available, water is heated by fossil or nuclear fuel to produce steam for driving turbines linked in turn to generators.

Using modest generating equipment which was installed in huts or basements, electricity was initially produced for public lighting — of streets (until then lit by gas, if at all), the exteriors of buildings and football grounds. The illumination was too intense for interior use until the vacuum filament lamp was invented, virtually simultaneously by Joseph Swan in Britain and Thomas Alva Edison in the USA — the two pioneers eventually joined forces in 1883. The first building to be lit entirely by electricity was the new Savoy Theatre in the Strand, London which was built in 1881 to the designs of C. J. Phipps for the impresario Richard D'Oyley Carte of Savoy Operas fame. The House of Commons was another early beneficiary.

The first 'power station' to supply power for distribution was at Godalming, a Surrey town then of 2,000 inhabitants south of Guildford which, in the words of a contemporary issue of *Engineering* magazine, found itself 'in the forefront of the contest of the electric light versus gas'. In September 1881 the local gas company's contract for lighting the town expired and the authorities decided to let the new technology show what it could do, using the water power of the River Wey which had a drop of 1.5m (5ft) at that point. The firm of Calder and Barrett accordingly came to an agreement with Messrs R. and J. Pulmans, a firm of leather dressers who used a water mill to drive their machinery, to install a Siemens generator in their premises, which were to be lit as part of the deal. However, this pioneering venture which linked the oldest and newest power sources, was not a great success and had to be backed up by an auxiliary steam engine. In 1882 the Edison company opened the world's first power station to supply external commercial premises in the basement of no 57 Holborn Viaduct, City of London, with machinery specially designed by Thomas Edison. Using ducts running below street level, this supplied current which was used originally for lighting the city's streets, and later in the Central Criminal Court of Justice at the Old Bailey, the

128

General Post Office, the City Temple (the first church to be electrically lit) and individual businesses.

A decisive moment for the infant industry came in 1883 when Sir Coutts Lindsay, the properietor of the Grosvenor Gallery in New Bond Street in the West End of London, decided not only to light his own premises with electricity but to accede to his neighbours' requests that he should supply them as well. Lindsay accordingly installed two of the largest Siemens generators available on the market and invited a young engineer of Italian descent, Sebastian Ziani de Ferranti, who had set up a business manufacturing electrical equipment, to come and run the station. De Ferranti increased the size and efficiency of the plant to the point where, within three years, it was supplying customers throughout central London. The journal *Industries* commented that it had 'in the fullest sense of the term been a pioneer in the public supply of electricity'.

Using his experience at the Grosvenor Gallery, de Ferranti next proposed a power station large enough to supply the whole of London and persuaded Lindsay and others to form the London Electric Supply Corporation Ltd to take over the gallery plant and build the new station, with de Ferranti as chief engineer. The company found a 1.2ha (3 acre) site on the banks of the Thames at Deptford, south-east London. The 'Stowage', as it was known, had previously been the stores of the East India Company (see page 103, Offices) and offered two important advantages: supplies of coal could be unloaded directly off the river, and there was ample cooling water available for condensing the steam from the turbines back into water.

Deptford began producing electricity in 1889. The lineal ancestor of the modern station, it was the first in Britain capable of generating power on a modern scale, and the prototype for the high-pressure AC system of distribution pioneered by de Ferranti which has subsequently become standard throughout the world. The current was carried at a pressure of 10,000 volts through insulated copper mains laid along railway lines and tunnels to distribution stations where it was reduced in voltage for local transmission. De Ferranti designed the entire station, buildings and machinery, working and often sleeping in a small cottage which stood on the site and earning himself the title of 'the Michelangelo of the installation'.

Deptford was designed with sufficient capacity to light the whole of London. The boiler and engine houses occupied a total area of 64 by 59.5m (210 by 195ft) and were nearly 30.5m (100ft) tall at their highest. In the words of a contemporary issue of *The Engineer*, construction was '. . . with the exception of the roof boarding . . . solely of iron, stone, concrete and brick . . . it will be, when in full working order, the largest . . . station in existence'.

The boilers, manufactured by Babcock and Willcock, were mounted in the boiler house on two floors 1m (3ft) apart, the upper supported on iron columns; above was a second floor, similarly supported and capable of carrying 4,000 tonnes of fuel which was supplied by chutes to the levels below. The station was extended in 1929–32 ('Deptford West') and again (after nationalisation in 1948) in 1953–7. The entire complex closed in 1983, marking the end of the era

Plate 38 Deptford, Britain's first modern power station. *(Central Electricity Generating Board)*

of local generation which, over the previous two decades, had been progressively replaced by the National Grid.

After lighting, transportation was the second major commercial application of electricity. The City and South London Railway of 1890 (see page 141, Railway Stations) was the world's first purpose-built underground electric railway, and many of the power stations were built or dedicated to supply power for railway companies and the tramway networks of local authorities. But the electrification of industry progressed relatively slowly. At the beginning of the 1920s half the factories in Britain remained without electricity, and industrial consumption ran at only 2,514 million units out of the 4,295 million generated by public stations. Ten years later industrial consumption had increased to 5,164 million units (out of 10,676 million generated) but there were still 30,000 factories (20 per cent of the total) relying on older sources of energy for power and sometimes lighting.

A crucial factor in the spread of electrification was the development of the National Grid. For the first time this allowed electricity to be fed by transmission lines to wherever it was needed, directly from the sites where it could be generated most efficiently (for example, in the coal-burning power stations of the Midlands). The Grid was built following the Electricity Supply Act of 1926 which came into force at a time when Britain's towns were being supplied by no fewer than 438 different power stations of varying levels of output and efficiency — rural areas hardly benefitted at all. The Grid became fully commercially operational in 1935, although until 1938 this was on a regional rather than a wholly national basis.

POWER STATIONS

The Central Electricity Board (later the Central Electricity Generating Board) was given the responsibility for co-ordinating the generation and distribution of electricity, and under its auspices the Grid developed and grew into the world's largest unified system of electricity generation and transmission. As regards the location of industry, the implications were dramatic. To quote L. T. C. Rolt in *Victorian Engineering*:

> For the first time, the location of power-consuming industries need no longer be confined to the coalfields of the Midlands and the North where fuel was cheap. Industry forsook the area which had cradled it and followed the marching pylons into the southern centres of England to establish itself in towns which the impact of the Industrial Revolution had hitherto but lightly touched.

The creation of the Grid (which was supplemented by a Supergrid of higher-voltage lines after nationalisation) set the scene for a new generation of higher-capacity stations and the decommissioning of hundreds of older ones — not only small and inefficient stations, but also such monuments of industrial

Plate 39 Calder Hall, the earliest nuclear power station with, (background), hyperbolic cooling towers of the kind first built in Britain in 1925. *(British Nuclear Fuels Ltd)*

architecture as Deptford, and Battersea in south-west London which was built in two stages (1929–35 and 1944–55) with Sir Giles Gilbert Scott as architectural consultant. The largest brick building in the world, Battersea closed in 1983 and was bought with the intention to convert it into a 468,000 cu m (16.5 million sq ft) indoor entertainment complex.

The modern face of electricity generation is represented by Britain's nuclear power stations. The earliest industrial-scale nuclear installation in the world is at Calder Hall, Cumbria where the first of an eventual four reactors began supplying electricity to the National Grid in 1956. The reactors, where heat for making steam is produced by nuclear fission, are housed in cylindrical mild steel pressure vessels measuring some 21.5m (70½ft) high and 11.3m (37ft) in diameter and enclosed in thick protective concrete shields. Calder Hall, which was designed by the chief architect of the then Ministry of Works, now forms part of British Nuclear Fuels' site at Sellafield; as well as feeding the National Grid, it supplies all BNF's requirements for electricity and process steam, making Sellafield the first industrial complex in the world to make full use of nuclear energy. Britain currently has over one hundred power stations in use or under construction, seventeen of them nuclear. The nuclear stations provide one-fifth of Britain's total energy requirement.

COOLING TOWERS

Power generation needs constant supplies of cooling water to condense steam after it has passed through turbines. The most efficient method of effecting this away from coastal or riverside sites (which in any case can be vulnerable to environmental problems caused by discharging warmed water) is in cooling towers where the used water loses its heat through contact with a flow of air, and is then recycled. The earliest cooling towers were rectangular and made of timber, and could not be built safely to withstand wind pressures at heights greater than 21m (70ft) — this was lower than the ideal height of 30.5m (100ft) needed for uniform distribution of the water. They were also fire risks and had a short life-span, and engineers therefore began experimenting with more efficient designs in more durable materials.

The decisive breakthrough came in the 1920s in the Netherlands, where engineers evolved a design for a much larger circular tower built in reinforced concrete with a hyperbolic 'flask-shaped' profile. Based on principles employed by Gustav Eiffel in his Eiffel tower in Paris, this enabled towers to be built to a height of 36.5m (120ft) without the risk of shearing stresses in the shell; it also provided the largest possible cooling surface, and ensured a good draught of air. The success of the Dutch experiment led to its introduction in Britain, where the earliest hyperbolic concrete cooling towers were erected in 1925 at Liverpool Corporation's Lister Drive power station. They were designed by consulting engineers L. G. Mouchel and Partners, using the French Hennebique system of reinforced concrete construction, and in conformity with the regulations for reinforced concrete structures as laid down by the then London County Council, which appeared to be the most relevant specification then available.

The Lister Drive towers were 40m (130ft) high with a base diameter of 30.5m (100ft) and with concrete shells varying in thickness between 305mm (12in) and 116mm (4.5in). Each was designed to cool 2.12 million litres (467,000 gallons) of water. They were demolished in 1972; but Liverpool's initiative had been rapidly followed, and the hyperbolic concrete cooling tower has become a familiar landmark. Despite their height, these structures bring something of the gracefulness of the potter's or glassblower's craft into a heavy industrial setting — a perfect example of function creating art.

PYLONS

The electricity industry has given the landscape a second new structure: the pylon, which carries the National Grid's transmission lines. Its arrival was controversial: some opposed it, for others it symbolised progress. Herbert Morrison was a politician who played a major role in the nationalisation of the industry; a member of the post-1945 Labour cabinet, he considered it favourably and saw 'a network of transmission lines and their pylons with a sense of majesty of their own, marching over many miles of country, giving a sense of power in the service of the people'. The poet Rudyard Kipling was also lyrical about the new landmarks:

> Braced, bolted, barred and stayed,
> and singing like the morning stars
> for joy that they are made.

Less enthusiastic were the property owners whose land the pylons would cross. But anticipating the reaction in the countryside, the Central Electricity Board engaged a prominent architect, Sir Reginald Blomfield, to advise on design. Blomfield chose an American model and modified it to achieve better proportions with a broader base and gantries in three tiers. The pylons were designed to be spaced at approximately 274m (900ft) intervals to give the transmission lines the same kind of graceful catenary curve as in the cables of a suspension bridge. The original Grid comprised 6,400km (4,000 miles) of transmission lines and 237 connecting substations linked by pylons, the first of which was erected near Edinburgh, Scotland in July 1928 and the last near Fordingbridge, Hampshire in September 1933.

PRISONS

The original purpose of prisons was not primarily to punish offenders but to detain them prior to their trial and the summary punishment that followed — in the form of execution, flogging or mutilation — for those found guilty. An early prison, therefore, needed to be no more elaborate than a cellar or a secure building such as a gatehouse. By the time of Alfred the Great, however, imprisonment had progressed to being a punishment in its own right, and a legal code introduced in about AD890 refers to incarceration as the penalty for failure to meet obligations. The Normans added to the number and security of prisons by the simple expedient of building castles (see page 61, Fortresses and military buildings), which provided as secure a means of keeping prisoners detained as they did of keeping attackers out. While castles fulfilled mainly military needs, only the more important prisoners were kept in turrets or special cells since the rest could safely languish in temporary timber huts in the castle yard.

But as the defensive rôle of castles diminished they were obvious candidates as more permanent prisons. A royal decree of 1166 made sheriffs — the principal law enforcement officers of the day — responsible for building gaols for those counties which did not possess them in royal boroughs or castles. The new gaols were mostly of timber until the late thirteenth century, when more durable materials such as stone or brick were used. Castles have served as gaols for centuries; a contributor to *Building News* in 1857, arguing against the adoption of modern designs, wrote that '. . . castle, since the days of the Normans, has, in the ears of the people, stood for prison for many a hundred years'. They are the oldest surviving buildings in Britain to have been used as prisons: Lancaster Castle remains one to this day and the Tower of London housed enemies of the State as recently as World War II. The oldest London building erected specifically as a prison was the Fleet, which may have dated from as early as the Conquest although it first enters recorded history in the twelfth century.

Outside London the network of sheriffs' prisons remained in being as county gaols until 1878, and formed the mainstay of the country's penal system. Other prisons were owned by boroughs or noblemen (including ecclesiastics) although it was eventually decreed that they should all come under the authority of the sovereign as instruments of the administration of justice. Until the eighteenth century gaols were not planned on any specific architectural or social principle, even when externally they were as monumental as the Debtors' Prison at York Castle, completed in 1705. Most were variations on the theme of contemporary town houses, with large rooms in which prisoners lived communally — only in the smaller local gaols was there any degree of privacy respected in living arrangements.

By that time the system was a mixture of county and municipal gaols, whose principal rôle was still to hold felons awaiting trial; debtors' prisons — debtors accounted for some 50 per cent of the total imprisoned population; 'bridewells', or houses of correction run by local magistrates for the disciplining of petty offenders; private prisons; and the London gaols which were the responsibility of the Crown. Not until 1877 were all prisons in the country put into the hands of a single body of prisoner commissioners. Conditions generally were appalling. Prisons were crowded with as many as thirty to a room, unsupervised, insanitary, corruptly run (thanks to the practice of tendering their management to private contractors who charged inmates for services) and quite inadequate to deal with a rising tide of criminal activity. The pressure was such that the government was coming to rely increasingly on the transportation of convicted criminals, initially to the American colonies until the Revolution of 1776, and then — from 1787 — to Australia, which was being colonised following the voyages of Captain Cook.

Transportation had been introduced during the reign of James I, and by 1770 there were ten transportations for every execution. When it was discontinued, it caused a crisis of overcrowding and the first response of the government was to use hulks — redundant sailing ships moored in estuaries as floating prisons where convicts were set to work on dredging and embankment building. But the high death rates sustained in the hulks ensured that they were only a temporary expedient and made it imperative to find a lasting solution to the problem of dealing with offenders. This emerged in the form of the penitentiary or purpose-built prison, as envisaged by the Penitentiary Act of 1779 which made imprisonment an alternative to transportation. The period when this more drastic penalty had been suspended — and during which the prison population had nearly doubled — provided the perfect conditions for the penal reform movement which was to sweep away the country's motley collection of prisons (in buildings ranging from castles to cottages, stables and cellars) and replace them with a new generation of gaols planned on the principle of individual cells, and designed with the twin social purposes of deterrence and the reform of character.

The prime instigator of the movement was John Howard who was appointed Sheriff of Bedfordshire in 1773 and did not like the conditions he found in his own county gaol. He set out on a series of journeys during the 1770s and 1780s and visited every gaol in England and Wales; he also went abroad to Europe, where he visited prisons in Flanders and Italy such as the Rome House of Correction for children (completed in 1704) which were built on the cell principle. In 1774 he gave evidence before Parliament on the first two Acts concerned with improving the treatment of prisoners, and three years later published the first edition of his *State of the Prisons* (the last and most complete version of which appeared in 1792) — a dry, factual account of the universally bad and unhealthy conditions in existing gaols (he even condemned London's newly completed Newgate) which was to influence the design and construction of prisons for the next century and a half. He argued for segregation (by age, sex and nature of crime), individual confinement in cells, and the employment of properly paid staff.

The first prison to be purpose-built in the spirit of the reform movement was the new county gaol at Horsham, West Sussex where Howard had visited the existing establishment in 1774, during an escape attempt! Within a year a 0.8ha (2 acre) plot of land was bought in East Street in the centre of the town and a design produced by a local architect, William Ride. The cell block was built of stock brick on foundations of local stone, with individual cells arranged on either side of a central corridor on the two upper floors over an arcaded ground storey; there were separate sections for male debtors and felons and for women prisoners, and rooms for the turnkey (warder). Work began soon afterwards on an infirmary, and on a governor's house and chapel; the entire group of buildings, with its surrounding wall, was completed in 1779. Howard visited the gaol in 1782 and found it 'as quiet as a private house . . . clean, healthy and well regulated'.

The example of Horsham, which continued in use until its demolition in 1845 (a railway line now passes through the site), was not widely followed at first because of expectations among the county authorities that the government was about to embark on its own building programme of new penitentiaries. The resumption of transportation, however, delayed the start on the first of these at Millbank, Westminster until 1811. Designed by William Wilkins and Thomas Hardwick on a 2.8ha (7 acre) site, Millbank was planned as the largest prison

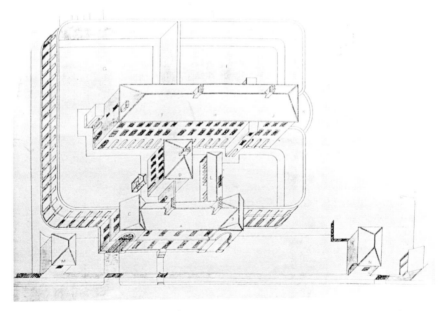

Plate 40 Horsham county gaol, Sussex,1831. A. Governor's house; B. Chapel; C. Gateway; D. Infirmary; E. Well house; F. Debtors' prison; G.Debtors' yard; H. Felons' prison; I. Felons' yard; J. Female felons; K. Female felons' yard; L. Hard labour machine; M. Coal store; N. Stables and yard. *(West Sussex County Council)*

in Europe, with room for over 1,000 convicts living and working in solitary confinement in individual cells. Completed in 1821 at a cost of nearly £500,000, it was intended to exemplify the 'panopticon' principle advocated in 1791 by the utilitarian philosopher Jeremy Bentham, and first adopted in the Edinburgh Bridewell completed in 1795 to the designs of Robert Adam.

A panopticon was built on a circular or semicircular plan with the inmates housed in radial blocks which could be supervised from a central control point. Bentham took the idea from a circular textile factory which his younger brother had built in the 1780s on the estate of a Russian prince for the same reason — to afford a high degree of visual surveillance. Radial planning also became the basic principle of nineteenth-century prisons in the USA. As built, Millbank was an extremely complicated structure, its plan one of radiating polygons instead of wings. The marshy site caused structural problems both before and after the arrival of the first convicts (from Newgate) in 1816, and the entire convict population had to be evacuated after an outbreak of disease in the 1820s. By 1890, when it was finally closed, Millbank was seen as an isolated and not particularly successful experiment in prison design; demolished in 1903 and replaced by Wormwood Scrubs, its site is now partly occupied by the Tate Gallery.

The true ancestor of the modern prison is Pentonville, completed in 1842 in Islington, north London and still in use. It was designed by Sir Joshua Jebb, a military engineer who became Britain's first Surveyor-General of Prisons, as a model establishment for incorporating the by-now accepted principle of separate quarters, for the newly appointed prison inspectorate set up by the government. Built to accommodate 520 convicts, Pentonville was laid out in a semicircular plan with four blocks radiating out from the central building. Each block contained three tiers of cells ranged on either side of its long walls and opening onto iron galleries under a barrel-vaulted roof. The cell in which the convict spent most of his time measured 2.1 by 4.0 by 2.7m (7 by 13 by 9ft) high and contained its own water supply, lavatory, gas light and ducted heating and ventilation. It was also designed to be as soundproof as possible, to prevent convicts communicating easily and to encourage reflection, and acoustic experiments were carried out at Millbank. Meals were served through traps in the cell doors and even during the short periods when they were outside their cells prisoners were kept incommunicado, by partitions in the chapel and by masks in the exercise courtyards between the blocks.

Pentonville served as the model for some fifty new prisons built over the next two decades, the plans for all of which had to be authorised by the surveyor-general. The principle of cell separation became compulsory in 1865 and in 1877 all gaols came under the unified administration of a newly established Prison Commission. The Victorian prisons built during this unprecedented wave of construction activity have continued to serve the needs of the British penal system until today and, although the principle of isolation was abolished in the interwar period, no comparable twentieth-century building programme has been attempted.

RAILWAY STATIONS

More than any other event of the Industrial Revolution the coming of the railways signalled the dawn of the modern world. They brought mobility to the mass of the population, removed the need for people to live close to their work, enabled manufacturers to distribute their goods rapidly and nationally and created the tourist trade. These possibilities, admittedly, were not foreseen by the early promoters of railways who viewed them as a way of moving goods rather than people; the Stockton and Darlington line, for example, opened in 1825 primarily to transport coal. Specialised buildings were not needed for goods traffic and the earliest railway buildings were existing sheds and warehouses with a house built or acquired for the agent who supervised operations.

It did not take long, however, for the railways to appreciate the potential for the movement of people. Some early lines used conveniently situated coaching inns and hotels; but from its inception the Liverpool and Manchester company included plans to carry passengers, and built the first two purpose-built railway stations in the world as the twin termini of the earliest regular rail passenger route, which opened in 1830. The service was an immediate success and within a year was carrying over 2,000 passengers a day between the two cities. The original Liverpool terminus, at Crown Street, proved too remote from the city centre and was soon replaced by Lime Street which is still the main Liverpool railhead. The Manchester station at Liverpool Road, off Deansgate, closed to passenger traffic in 1844 when the terminus moved to Hunts Bank (now Victoria), but continued in use as a goods depot until 1975.

Unusually among early station buildings it survives, together with a group of warehouses which were built at the same time on the opposite side of the rails. The architect, who was probably also responsible for the Liverpool terminus, is unknown; but the likeliest possibility is Thomas Haigh of the Liverpool firm of Haigh and Franklin. The station is a two-storey domestic-scale building with a 24.4m (80ft) long frontage onto Liverpool Road. Of brick construction, it is faced with stucco, the lower storey in a strongly rusticated finish to present what a contemporary commentator called a 'Grecian front'. There were separate street entrances to the first- and second-class booking offices, each with its own waiting room above, which was reached by a private staircase. The railway line entered at high level after crossing bridges over the River Irwell and Water Street.

The station stands in a terrace of railway buildings. To the east is a three-storeyed brick house built in 1809 for a partner in dyeworks whose premises were acquired by the railway company; it became the station agent's house. To the west the company built, in a similar style to the station, first a

Plate 41 Liverpool Road station, Manchester, with (from left) the earlier agent's house and the station building itself. Off the photograph to the right is the range of shops with carriage sheds above them. *(Greater Manchester Museum of Science and Industry)*

carriage and parcels offices and then a row of shops which were rented out until they were needed as engineering and joinery workshops to service the railway. The apparent upper storey over the shops is merely a façade — behind it lay covered accommodation for twenty passenger carriages. The whole complex survives in good condition and is now part of the Greater Manchester Museum of Science and Industry.

Modest though it was, Liverpool Road contained from the outset all the essential elements of the railway station and these reappeared in the earliest London stations which were built over the next decade. The first permanent terminus in London opened in 1836 at London Bridge, the City end of the suburban London and Greenwich Railway. In its original form it had two uncovered platforms and a separate three-storey office block at the end of the 5.6km (3.5 mile) long viaduct of brick arches which carried the line at rooftop level. Nothing of the early structure survives, however, and the site has been rebuilt more than once in its 150-plus years of history as a terminus, most recently in 1978.

London's first main-line terminus was Euston which opened in 1837, a few months after London Bridge, and was situated at the southern end of the London and Birmingham Railway. Initially passengers simply arrived at and departed from the purely functional iron and glass-roofed trainshed designed by the railway engineer Robert Stephenson, but the railway company had plans for something a good deal more ambitious for the world's earliest long-distance railway line, and called in Philip Hardwick as architect. Hardwick produced a suitably dramatic entrance, completed in 1840, its centrepiece a great Doric portico of Yorkshire stone through which passengers in their carriages passed as through the solemn gateway of one of the great metropolises of ancient history.

Between this portal and the train shed, Hardwick and his son Philip C. Hardwick, later built the Great Hall (completed in 1849) which served as the main passenger concourse until the 1960s when the entire group of buildings was swept away — this provoked especial indignation in the case of the portico, which could easily have been preserved; it made room for the present-day Euston, designed by British Rail architects on the anonymous principles of the modern airport terminal, and opened in 1968. It is a sad contrast with its predecessor, which at the time of its building demonstrated how quick the railway companies were — in the words of architectural writer Harold Brockman — in

taking up their aesthetic responsibilities, with great earnestness, for it was prestige which counted . . . Hardwick's magnificent Doric gateway of 1840 stood astride the station entry . . . a symbol for the classic school of railway architects which followed.

The demise of Euston leaves King's Cross as the oldest substantially unaltered London terminus. The station was completed in 1852, its design a collaborative venture by the Cubitt dynasty of Sir William, the engineer to the Great Northern Railway, and his sons Joseph (engineer) and Lewis (architect). Simple and modern in appearance, its front elevation is a screen of London stock brick pierced by two huge, semicircular openings which echo the roofs of the twin train sheds behind. King's Cross was followed by Paddington, which was completed in 1854 by Isambard Kingdom Brunel, the engineer to the Great Western Railway, and the architect Matthew Digby Wyatt — and over the rest of the nineteenth century by the rest of the London termini, ending with Marylebone in 1899. In the regions, the earliest surviving mainline stations include Brunel's Bristol Temple Gate, completed in 1841 and subsequently superseded by Temple Meads; and Newcastle Central, begun in 1848 with John Dobson as architect. By this time, stations were eloquently displaying in their construction the emerging rivalry between architects (in the station buildings and hotels) and civil engineers (in the trainsheds and approaches) in producing dramatic architectural effects.

UNDERGROUND

Underground railways were introduced in the second half of the nineteenth century in response to the growing urban congestion of London and Glasgow. The first underground in the world opened in London in 1863 and ran a distance of 6km (3.75 miles) between Paddington and Farringdon Street, with intermediate stations at Edgware Road, Baker Street, Great Portland Street, Euston Square and King's Cross. The route followed the line of streets as far as possible. Construction was by the 'cut and cover method' in which a trench was dug to track-bed level and then covered with brick arches on which a new road surface was laid, leaving the trains running just below the streets. The stations could all be reached by short staircases, and were designed by the engineer to the line, Sir John Fowler with the help of Sir Benjamin Baker; they were later to work together on the City and South London Railway.

The original terminals were in open cuttings with glass roofs (the supporting brackets can still be seen at Paddington) while the intermediate stations were covered by brick-arched ceilings pierced along the platform walls by shafts for natural lighting — an effect which has been re-created in the restoration of Baker Street. All the stations with the exception of the initial King's Cross are still in use; the platforms at Baker Street, Great Portland Street and Euston Square are the original ones, although none of the early street-level station buildings survives. The line was extended at both ends during the 1860s and now forms part of London Underground's Metropolitan and Circle system.

The world's first deep-level tube railway, and the first to use electric traction, opened in 1890 between King William Street in the City, and Stockwell, south of the River Thames — a distance of 5.5km (3.5 miles). There were intermediate stations at Borough, Elephant & Castle, Kennington and Oval where the platforms were formed by widening the running tunnels; they were reached by lifts. The original street-level buildings were single storey, domed structures designed by Thomas Phillips Figgis — the listed Kennington is the most characteristic survival. Bank later replaced King William Street as the City terminus, and its original classical entrances are still in use on either side of the Church of St Mary Woolnoth. The City and South London Railway, as it was known, now forms part of London Underground's Northern Line.

The first underground system built in a single operation is the Glasgow subway, a circular line which opened in 1896 to provide better connections between the north and south banks of the River Clyde; it has now been completely reconstructed. The original stations were typically islands of timber construction with insignificant street level entrances; the exception, which still survives is St Enoch, which a contemporary report in *Building* described as 'a doll's house beside its big neighbour' (the St Enoch terminus, now demolished) but 'simply charming'.

SHOPPING ARCADES

Enclosed shopping has a long history. Both in the warm climates of the Mediterranean and in cooler, rainier ones such as Britain's, it made sense to provide people shopping with protection from the elements. The Greeks and Romans built shops behind arcades and colonnades for coolness, and the tradition revived with the Renaissance rediscovery of classical ideas. Arcading became the accepted form of street enclosure, spreading north during the sixteenth century, and the earliest exchanges (see page 44, Exchanges and financial markets) were of this pattern. London's first Royal Exchange was built in 1568 on similar lines to the Antwerp Bourse, and comprised a galleried courtyard building with one hundred shops and booths, the rents from which were intended to pay for the whole development. Gresham's enterprise encouraged similar developments during the following century, notably the New Exchange of 1608 and the later Exeter 'Change (see page 163, Zoos), both in the Strand.

But Britain had already developed its own local traditions of planned and at least partly enclosed shopping. The most unusual medieval survival is the Rows at Chester which consists of two-tier parades of shops with their upper levels set back behind covered walkways; they flank the main shopping streets which radiate from the centre of the city at Chester Cross. Chester was a Roman legionary headquarters, and their grid layout survives in the town's present-day street pattern; one theory of the origin of the Rows is that they were first built over the remains of Roman shops, possibly as a safeguard against looting by Welsh raiders. Their continuous history dates at least from the thirteenth-century rebuilding of the city after its devastation by fire, and the existing documentary evidence dates from this period. Another historical strand comes with the market hall — during the Tudor period towns would commonly express their growing prosperity by building guild or town halls above an arcaded area for the use of market traders (see page 89, Markets).

But none of these precedents produced as successful an approach to enclosed shopping as the indoor street that takes its name from its arcaded predecessors. This arrived in Britain in the early nineteenth century and was designed to provide for the luxury end of what we now call comparison shopping. In its strictly defined sense — of a pedestrian shopping street covered with a fully or partly glazed roof — the arcade originated in pre-revolutionary Paris, where the 'Galerie du Bois' formed one side of Victor Louis' quadrangle of shops, apartments, cafés and restaurants, built in 1781–6. This was replaced in 1828 by the Galerie d'Orléans, by which time British visitors returning from France were bringing back reports of this new and convenient way in which to shop.

The modern arcade was a brilliant innovation. It gave fashionable shoppers a comfortable and well-lit environment in which to browse for fashion goods and to meet their friends; it protected them from the weather and, not least, from the filthy condition of the city streets of the time. The first built in Britain was the Royal Opera Arcade which runs between Pall Mall and Charles II Street in the West End of London. Opened in 1817 and designed by John Nash and George Repton, it formed part of the great metropolitan improvement in which Nash, the favourite architect of the Prince Regent (later George IV), designed Regent Street as the centrepiece of the new West End, with a covered colonnade along the curve of the Quadrant. The Royal Opera Arcade was financed by the Crown Estate and is a fairly modest example of the type characterised by circular rooflights and relatively plain street entrances; it has seventeen bow-fronted Regency shops which lie along the western side only, and was initially planned as the covered approach to the new Royal Opera House which Nash and Repton designed in 1813. Their opera house burned down in 1864, and its successor was pulled down in 1891 and replaced by the present Her Majesty's Theatre and a hotel, the Carlton. The Carlton was replaced in turn in 1963 by New Zealand House where, as part of the development, a ground-floor banking hall and shops were allowed to pierce the previously blank eastern wall of the arcade at the southern end.

Within a year it had inspired the much larger and perennially successful Burlington Arcade, designed by Samuel Ware for Lord Burlington, which opened in 1818. Over the next forty years the new fashion in shopping was adopted with enthusiasm by cities and resort towns throughout the country — the earliest built outside London were in Bristol (1824), Bath (1825), Glasgow (1827), Newcastle-upon-Tyne (1832), Ryde, Isle of Wight (1835), Glossop, Derbyshire (1838), Cheltenham (1845) and Cardiff (1858). Their popularity was assisted by the increased availability of glass, which meant they could be naturally lit through glazed roofs and that shopkeepers could display their wares to good effect to passing customers. From 1832 onwards, sheet glass was being produced in Britain in economically sized panes (see page 51, Exhibition centres), and the abolition of taxes on glass by 1845 meant that it could be used as a construction material on a large scale for the first time in Britain.

New arcades continued to open throughout the nineteenth and early twentieth centuries, and over a hundred survive. A number have been lost to unsympathetic redevelopment, but the importance of the arcade as good townscape and as a focus for quality shopping was fortunately recognised in time to prevent more damage, and some forty of the best examples (all dating from before 1930) are now statutorily protected by listing legislation. The historic arcade derived its charm and character from the smallness and intimacy of its individually owned shops and the quality of the goods which they sold — fashions, jewellery and the like. It remains a relevant architectural form which can be reproduced as a setting for specialist shops in urban redevelopment schemes such as Hays Galleria in London Bridge City, and the Marlowe Arcade at Canterbury.

SHOPPING MALLS

The concept of covered pedestrian shopping has also re-emerged in the late twentieth century in the quite different context of modern shopping centres, with their enclosed malls and courts. These were first built in the USA well before World War II, and were introduced into Britain in the 1960s as planned elements in the redevelopment of major town and city centres. As early as 1956, the then London County Council included provision for a substantial shopping complex on a 1.2ha (3 acre) site at the Elephant and Castle in south London, one of the first comprehensive development areas to be designated in Britain under post-World War II planning legislation.

The Elephant and Castle Centre, which opened in May 1965, is based on a cruciform pattern of intersecting malls. Its architects were Boissevain & Osmond who, with developers the Willett Group, came top out of thirty-six entrants in the LCC's competition. Their proposal provided 18,770sq m (202,000sq ft) of shopping, in a 146 by 67m (480 by 220ft) box of reinforced concrete construction faced in metal cladding panels. The shops ranged along the intersecting malls, originally on three levels with the upper two in the form of a great double-height, glass-roofed arcade; however, the effect of this has largely been lost by the conversion, in the 1970s, of the topmost floor which was never commercially successful — it became a conference centre for the Department of Health and Social Security, occupier of the tower-block rising over the Centre. The winning design was commended in the *Architects' Journal* for 21 July 1960 as being 'outstanding . . . not least in its imaginative return to the covered arcade as a comfortable and convenient arrangement.

This reinvention of the arcade occurred a year after the first modern enclosed shopping centre opened in Britain. By 1960, when the LCC was inviting bids for the opportunity to build the Elephant and Castle, Birmingham City Council had already sought proposals for the redevelopment of the city's historic Bull Ring markets area, a 1.6ha (4 acre) site next to New Street Station which took its name from a medieval bull-baiting arena. In February of that year the Council selected, as the best of eleven submissions, Laing Developments' scheme for a 32,520sq m (350,000sq ft) complex of enclosed malls and courts on several levels. Designed by Laing Developments' chief architect Sidney Greenwood in association with T. J. Hirst, the Bull Ring was an irregular polygon in plan which made no attempt to re-create the arcade; it was built of reinforced concrete clad with precast concrete panels.

During the formulation of their scheme, Laing studied North American shopping centres and found that their suburban locations offered little in the way of precedents for a complex which had to be fitted onto a confined site in the heart of a major city. In the words of *Official Architecture and Planning* for July 1964, there was 'no comparable downtown shopping development on the scale

Plate 42 The Royal Opera Arcade, oldest in Britain. *(Crown estates commissioners; photograph by Chris Morris)*

Plate 43 The Elephant and Castle shopping centre, south London, was seen as the rebirth of the arcade in a modern context. The photograph was taken before the uppermost floor was converted to a conference centre. *(Land Securities Properties Ltd)*

of the Bull Ring Centre, either in America or elsewhere'. Completed at a cost of £8 million, the Bull Ring opened in the spring of 1964 and was hailed as a blueprint for modern city-centre shopping. In 1987 it was acquired by the London and Edinburgh Trust who, in consultation with Birmingham City Council, produced proposals for a replacement 92,900sq m (1,000,000sq ft) centre on three levels, designed by Chapman Taylor Partners.

Despite a slow start for the Elephant and Castle, both centres succeeded in demonstrating the potential for providing enclosed shopping on the grand scale and were followed by a stream of new complexes; all of them were situated in existing towns until 1972 when planning approval was finally secured (after an eight-year struggle) for the Brent Cross edge-of-town development in north-west London. It was intended as an alternative to the West End with its concentration of department and multiple stores, and supermarkets ranged along covered malls, and offered 73,000sq m (790,000sq ft) of shopping, with 5,600 parking spaces and its own bus station at the junction of three major roads. Opened in 1976, it was designed by architects the Bernard Engle Partnership for the Hammerson Property and Investment Trust, and is the earliest example in Britain of the free-standing, decentralised shopping centre which has been familiar in North America for decades.

Brent Cross, in turn, triggered off a series of proposals for new enclosed shopping centres in edge-of-town or wholly out-of-town locations, designed for car-borne shoppers and therefore providing ample surface parking. The most spectacular of these is the MetroCentre at Gateshead, Tyneside, which opened in 1988; it is the largest shopping centre in Europe, and represents a further movement in the direction of American-style retailing by being the first in Britain to incorporate a purpose-designed 'leisure box' in the form of MetroWorld, an indoor funfair. (MetroWorld was conceived by the originators of West Edmonton Mall in Alberta, Canada.)

Thus while the original arcades were designed for the select few, their modern successors have popularised present-day mall shopping with supermarkets, department stores and retail multiples as 'anchors', in addition to speciality shops. According to the Unit for Retail Planning Information, Britain now has over 250 managed shopping centres with a minimum area of 9,290sq m (100,000sq ft).

SPORTS CENTRES

Indoor sports centres which contain one or more large, unobstructed enclosed playing areas, are the most recent of all the building types described in this book, with a history — as far as community use is concerned — going back no further than the 1960s. The general assumption until then had been that sport was an out-of-doors event, with no more facilities necessary than the pavilions, changing rooms and accommodation for spectators which individual sports clubs and teams had been providing for the previous hundred years and more. Special buildings for sport therefore, with the exception of swimming, were not considered to be a necessary public or commercial service to the community. This attitude was challenged by the 1960 Wolfenden Report on Sport and the Community which surveyed the condition of, and provision for, sport in Britain and produced a series of recommendations for action. Its key conclusion was that 'the most serious shortage is of facilities for the multitude of games and sports which, of their nature and in our climate, can best be played indoors'.

The first indoor sports hall built in Britain in fact antedated Wolfenden by seven years — but it was intended for serious athletes. This was the King George VI Hall which the Central Council for Physical Education (CCPE) — the predecessor of the modern Sports Council — built in 1953 at its national centre at Lillieshall, north-west of Wellington in Shropshire. Lillieshall Hall was built in 1830 as a country house for the Duke of Sutherland by Sir Jeffry Wyatville. The CCPE acquired the estate in 1951 and it has subsequently been developed with new buildings and outdoor facilities for sportsmen and women and their coaches.

Four years after Wolfenden had reported came the opening of Britain's first purpose-designed recreational sports centres: the National Recreation Centre in south London and the Sportcentre at Harlow, Essex. The NRC occupies a 14.5ha (36 acre) site in the grounds of the Crystal Palace exhibition building which was destroyed by fire in 1936 (see page 52, Exhibition centres). It was the inspiration of Sir Gerald Barry, the director of the 1951 Festival of Britain, who was invited to draw up recommendations for the future use of the land by the then London County Council, which took over responsibility for it from the government the same year. Sir Gerald drew attention to the anomaly that

> the British nation which invented and bequeathed to others most of the forms of sport which are now enjoyed throughout the Western world should have no central home for sport of their own . . . the existence of such a place would be likely to act as a sharp incentive to athletes and trainers throughout the country.

Plate 44 The Harlow Sportcentre in action, a quarter of a century after its opening. *(Harlow and District Sports Trust)*

His recommendation was adopted, and design work began in 1960 in the LCC's Department of Architecture and Civic Design (architect Sir Hubert Bennett in succession to Sir Leslie Martin). The facilities include an indoor arena 46 by 31m (151 by 101ft), training halls, sports pitches, athletics stadium, swimming pool hall, artificial ski slope, and a hostel for visitors training or playing in competitions. Crystal Palace is a national resource, providing a venue for international and national events, a training centre for national teams, coaches and serious enthusiasts as well as a starting point for complete beginners. The Harlow Sportcentre, on the other hand, is community-oriented, and was aimed from the outset at providing the missing link between outdoor and indoor sports facilities for whole families and for individuals who were players of very average abilities, or who wanted to try out a new sport. The formula which it pioneered has been adopted throughout the country.

The Harlow Sportcentre was introduced as an integral element in the development of Harlow, one of a ring of eight new towns created after the end of World War II to disperse people from overcrowded areas of London. Harlow, 40km (25 miles) north-east of the capital, was the fourth new town to be designated in 1947, and in 1955 the architects to its development corporation, Frederick Gibberd and Partners, drew up plans for a sports complex. This was traditionally based on a football and athletics stadium with pitches for other sports, and was located on a 12ha (30 acre) site in a green 'wedge' running between the town centre and the station. The stadium was completed in 1958, with terraces banked up using spoil from roadbuilding.

The following year saw the creation of the charitable Harlow and District Sports Trust to manage the facilities. In 1963 the Trust took the imaginative decision to put Wolfenden's recommendations into practice by building an enclosed sports hall with the aid of finance from, among others, the Development Corporation and the Wolfson Foundation. Designed by Frederick Gibberd and Partners, whose brief was to produce a tough, durable building at minimal cost, the Sportcentre opened in 1964 at a cost of £110,000. It is essentially a box built on a structural steel frame, with reinforced concrete floors and external walls of concrete blockwork and brick, and finished in aluminium sheeting, chosen for its economy and to give a light appearance to a large building. The ground floor is mostly taken up with the main sports hall which is 36.6 by 30.5m (120 by 100ft) and with a clear height of 8.5m (28ft). Around this are a practice hall,

Plate 45 The Billingham Forum Leisure Complex — the first in the country when it opened in 1967. It consists of sports halls, ice rink and swimming pools, as well as Teesside's top professional theatre. *(Stockton-on-Tees Borough Council)*

gymnasium, squash courts, changing rooms and refreshment areas.

The Sportcentre was a success from the start, and within less than a year was in use fourteen hours a day, seven days a week. In a 1967 appraisal, three years after it first opened, the *Architects' Journal* commented that 'the way the Sportcentre operates should serve as a model for other committees', and it has inspired a whole generation of indoor sports and leisure centres which have proliferated throughout Britain since the mid-1960s. By the end of that decade the first examples of sports halls combined with swimming pools were beginning to appear in towns like Basingstoke and Folkestone, while the first built for joint use by a school and the local community was at Bingham, Nottinghamshire. The first to combine sports provision with a theatre in a single town-centre building is the Billingham Forum in Teesside.

Completed in 1967, the Forum has been aptly described as the 'father of the British leisure centre'. Years ahead of its time, it was imaginatively conceived by the then Billingham Urban District Council to serve the wider population of Teesside, and was designed by Elder Lester and Partners as a place in which an entire family could enjoy their leisure hours, active or passive, cultural or sporting. Built for the remarkably low cost of £1 million, its four elements — an ice rink, a two-level sports hall, a 650-seater theatre and a swimming hall — form the four corners of a 91 by 82m (300 by 270ft) building, grouped round a restaurant and an internal courtyard which are positioned to encourage awareness of and experimentation with the full range of options. Externally, too, the building suggests a diversity of attractions by being explicitly broken up into its distinct elements and clad in a variety of materials — brickwork, blockwork, proprietary aluminium and glazing — which have the additional role of giving a visual focus to what was otherwise an uninteresting town centre. The ice rink is the largest single area with a clear span of 73m (240ft) and the capacity to accommodate 1,200 skaters at a time, and is particularly boldly expressed.

Since the 1960s, leisure has become an industry; in the 1970s it received a major boost as a result of the reorganisation of local government which set in train a nationwide building programme. This produced some 200 new sports and leisure centres in a three-year period; among them the first of the leisure pools, with the emphasis on family recreation rather than competitive ability.

TELEPHONY BUILDINGS

Telegraphy is defined as the use of electricity to send non-verbal messages over distances, and was in use by the 1830s. In 1839 the Great Western Railway laid the world's first commercial telegraph line between its London terminus at Paddington, and West Drayton (this was also the earliest commercial application of electricity). In 1850 the Electric Telegraph Company opened the world's first telegraphic exchange in Founders Court, Lothbury, in the City of London and the following year saw the first successful laying of an international submarine cable, between Britain and France. The greatest limitation to the telegraph was that although it could send signals — for example in the Morse code — it could not relay voiced communication. This had to wait until 1876 when the Scots-born Alexander Graham Bell patented a working telephone in Boston, Massachusetts after three years of research and experiment.

In 1878 Bell demonstrated his telephone before Queen Victoria and the same year saw the registration in London of The Telephone Company Ltd to exploit his patents. The company took space in an office building at no 36 Coleman Street in the City, and in the basement in August of the following year, opened the country's first public telephone exchange. On the mansard roof it built a metal framework to carry wires from the exchange to subscribers. By the end of 1879 the telephone company had opened two further exchanges, in office buildings in the City and in Westminster, to serve its 200 or so subscribers.

In the same year a rival company — the Edison Telephone Company of London — opened exchanges in the City to operate the rival system developed by Thomas Alva Edison. However, the two companies merged in 1880 as the United Telephone Company Ltd, and this produced an instrument combining the best features of the two patents and increased its network of London exchanges to eight by 1881 and about fifteen by the end of the following year. A description of an early exchange appeared in the 6 December 1883 edition of the *Pall Mall Gazette*.

What, then, is a telephone exchange station? We will take the East India Avenue in the City as an average sample. From the lofty roof of one of the houses of that sombre court rises a derrick, a square structure of wrought-iron bars 30 or 40 feet high by 8 or 10 feet wide [9 or 12m high by 2.4 or 3m wide]

Plate 46 The first telephone exchange at no 36 Coleman Street, in the City. (*Telecom Technology Showcase*)

and looking like the upper portion of a skeleton lighthouse, very rigid and very transparent. This edifice is surmounted by a lightning conductor; you ascend it by a perpendicular ladder, and, pausing on its upper storey — for it is divided into two floors — you look round from your airy perch to find that what appear innumerable wires radiate from your transparent cage in every possible direction over the dirty housetops of the City. Most of these wires are bare and unenclosed; others are in cables containing each twenty wires. Each of them is lettered and numbered, and a cupboard on the derrick contains an apparatus for testing them.

So much for what is above the roof. Below, in the attic, is a room occupied by eleven young ladies. The 271 wires, which represent the subscribers of the East India Avenue Exchange with 46 trunk and other direct wires, are guided down from the derrick above into neat mahogany cabinets or cases, in front of which the young ladies are seated. The alert dexterity with which at the signal given by the fall of a small lid about the size of a teaspoon the lady hitches on the applicant to the number with which he desires to talk is pleasant to watch. On the day of our visit there had been in this one office no less than 2,400 calls. Here, indeed, is an occupation to which no heavy father could object; and the result is that a higher class of young women can be obtained for the secluded career of a telephonist as compared with that which follows the more barmaid-like occupation of a telegraph clerk.

The new amenity spread rapidly to the provinces. In 1879 local companies opened exchanges in Manchester (in the Royal Exchange), Liverpool, Glasgow (at no 140 Douglas Street), Birmingham (Exchange Chambers), Edinburgh (St Andrew's Square) and Sheffield (in the premises of Taskers, rubber and leather merchants); the following year came Leeds (Royal Exchange) and Belfast (Castle Chambers). Typically, they were located in chambers and similar buildings which had been put up to house small businesses, until these proved inadequate for the needs of the new service. Moves were frequent in the early days: when the exchange at no 36 Coleman Street needed an improved switchboard it transferred to the Wood Street Exchange and eventually to London Wall where it occupied a building at nos 57/9 before being replaced by a new building following the introduction of subscriber trunk dialling in 1961.

From 1897 the National Telephone Company — which in 1899 was to take over the United and, with it, the London system — adopted a policy of adapting or constructing buildings specifically for telephony. It was not alone, for Parliament had established as early as 1880 that the independent telephone companies were to operate under licence from the Post Office. The PO, which had acquired all the private telegraph companies ten years earlier, was anxious to acquire an operational role in the new service and opened its own first exchange in 1881 in Swansea, South Wales.

In 1912 the PO acquired the National Telephone Company and, with it, 1,565 exchanges, over half a million subscribers and responsibility for all the country's telephone systems except for three operated by local authorities — of these only one survives, that run by the city of Kingston-upon-Hull in Humberside. Competition was reintroduced into Britain nationally by the 1981 Telecommunications Act which created British Telecom as a separate organisation as distinct from the Post Office. In 1986 Mercury Communications became an officially licensed competitor with British Telecom, and two years later installed the first of its public call boxes.

TELEPHONY IN THE SPACE AGE

By the 1960s the growth in international communications had set the scene for a new generation of telecommunications buildings, designed to make use of new developments in high-frequency microwave transmission and space technology. Britain's first earth-satellite station was completed at Goonhilly, on the Lizard peninsula in Cornwall, in July 1962, in time for the launch of the world's first orbiting communications satellite, Telstar. The original Goonhilly installation was designed by Husband and Co and consisted of a single, stainless-steel reflector dish aerial, 26m (85ft) in diameter, supported by a galvanised steel framework and mounted on a reinforced concrete base. The dish, with a total moving weight of 1,118 tonnes, was designed to rotate and tilt rapidly to focus on the early satellites which, unlike today's geo-stationary versions, were only intermittently within range.

Goonhilly now has ten dish aerials in use. Together with other British stations, including the Teleport in London's Docklands, it forms part of a worldwide satellite network handling two-thirds of all Britain's international telephone calls as well as television coverage of major world events, communications with ships at sea, and computer data. By the time that Goonhilly was operational, work had started on London's Telecom Tower. Designed by the Property Services Agency — the British government's construction arm — and completed in 1965, the Tower harnessed microwave technology to Britain's internal communications, so reducing the need for underground cabling. Microwaves travel in straight lines and with London lying in a valley the Tower — 189m (620ft) high — was necessary to ensure a clear path for signals being beamed over the city's skyline and the surrounding hills to other regional towers and (via satellite stations) international destinations. It transmits telephone conversations, networks television programmes and is a focal point for cellular radio.

PUBLIC PHONE BOXES

At the opposite end of the technological spectrum, the most characteristic telephone buildings in Britain are the public phone boxes, 83,000 of them. The pre-1912 companies produced a variety of designs ranging from the utilitarian to the picturesque in timber or iron, and it was not until 1921 that the Post Office introduced the first standard box, a rectangular cabinet of reinforced concrete. Three years later it held a competition for a better design in cast iron, which was won by Sir Giles Gilbert Scott. His K2 was installed from 1927 in London and major provincial cities; but it was his developed 'Jubilee' version (K6), introduced in 1936, which became a familiar sight in cities and villages

Plate 47 The telephone kiosk as historic building; Sir Giles Gilbert Scott's K2 is the oldest type still in use. *(British Telecommunications plc)*

throughout Britain. Common to both was their bright red paint, the small-paned windows and domed roof. The last two of these were abandoned in favour of the final variation on the historic design, K8, which arrived in 1968.

In 1985 British Telecom introduced a new, functional glass and aluminium kiosk to replace the K series in all but some 1,000 locations, where the traditional boxes are being preserved as buildings of special architectural and historic interest. British Telecom's competitor, Mercury Communications, chose to return to the design tradition in 1988 when it introduced its own public telephone boxes. In deliberate contrast with British Telecom's new kiosk Mercury commissioned no fewer than three styles: a Grecian pavilion with columns, by neo-classical architects John Simpson and Partners; a glazed canopy by conservatory specialists Machin Designs; and an art-deco totem pole by international designers Fitch and Co. The three types were all installed simultaneously at Waterloo Station, London, prior to the nationwide establishment of British's first alternative public telephone network.

THEATRES

During the Middle Ages drama was of two kinds, secular and religious. Secular displays were presented by roving bands of players using improvised premises: a cart in a market square, the yard of an inn, or a raised dais in the hall of a nobleman. Religious drama began in churches as an elaboration of liturgical services and blossomed into the full-blown mystery play cycles which eventually outgrew their original settings and came under the patronage of the town guilds. Individual scenes were played as 'pageants' on elaborate wagons grouped in an appropriate public space. Specific theatrical locations were unusual, although medieval Cornish villages built round stages, of earth or stone, up to 15m (50ft) in diameter; and the existence of a fourteenth-century theatre in Exeter, Devon is attested by virtue of an ecclesiastical order of 1384 which forbade, 'the performance of a certain harmful and blameworthy play or rather buffoonery in scorn and insult to the leather dressers and their craft . . . in the Theatre of our City'. But we have no description of this rarity.

By the sixteenth century, drama had matured into an art form which was recognisable as the ancestor of the modern theatre, served by a generation of playwrights unsurpassed in British history and by professional players who enjoyed the protection of noblemen and royalty — although they were harassed by the vagrancy laws which town and city authorities were applying with increasing severity. In London, they settled at first in inns such as the Boar's Head in Whitechapel and the Saracen's Head in Islington, as these were beyond the jurisdiction of the City Corporation; they soon became regular settings for plays. A galleried inn of the kind can still be seen in the George in Borough High Street, south London, which was built in 1676.

The first permanent theatre of which we have evidence was opened in 1576 (when Shakespeare was twelve years old) in open fields near Shoreditch, east London by James Burbage, the leader of a prominent troupe of players who had received his licence two years before from Queen Elizabeth I. Called simply 'The Theatre', it was built of timber and resembled the contemporary galleried inns and bull- and bear-baiting yards which were the natural venues for public entertainment. In the same year Richard Farrant, choirmaster of the Chapel Royal, converted a suite of rooms in a former monastic foundation at Blackfriars into a theatre where his charges could act plays before more select (and higher-paying) audiences. Like the earlier inns, both were outside the control of the City authorities. For the same reason most of the theatres which followed were built in Southwark, across the Thames from the City — such as the Rose, which was excavated in 1989 during preparatory site works for a new office block.

In 1595 the Swan opened here, the earliest post-medieval theatre in Britain of which we have a detailed description. A Dutchman called de Witt visited it within a year or so of its construction and sent a sketch to a friend of his called van Buchel. The Swan was a circular building three storeys high, its timber frame infilled with a 'concrete' of flint stones and covered with a thatched roof. In the centre was an open area, the pit, largely occupied by a platform stage measuring some 9 by 7m (30 by 23ft) and raised off the ground by trestles; early theatres were normally unroofed to provide maximum natural light for the action on stage. Halfway along its sides were two timber columns, painted to look like marble, which supported a sloping roof covering the rear portion. The yard in front was for standing spectators, the 'groundlings', who paid the lowest admission charge of one (old) penny (0.4p).

At the rear were the dressing rooms. Above the stage, and protected by a sloping roof, was a gallery of the kind that would be needed for the balcony scene in *Romeo and Juliet*. The underside of the stage roof was covered with a ceiling, and in the intervening void was machinery, used for the ascents and descents of gods and mythological beings, which continued upwards into a turreted hut above the gallery. In many early theatres like the Swan the stage, dressing room and machinery rooms were freestanding structures separate from the building enclosure, so that they could be dismantled for other kinds of entertainment.

The most famous theatre of this kind was the Globe, built in 1598 with timbers taken from the original theatre for William Shakespeare's acting company; burnt down in 1613 it was re-erected within a year. In 1988, construction work began on a replica Globe, on a site close to that of the original theatre.

Eight years after the first rebuilding of the Globe came the Banqueting House in Whitehall, Westminster, the earliest extant building in Britain designed with theatrical use at least partly in mind. It was completed in 1622 as a venue for state ceremonial occasions. Its architect, Inigo Jones, gained his early reputation as a designer of masques and stage sets and designed a building which was a perfect setting for the masques staged there until shortly before the Civil War. However, the puritanical Protectorate which followed brought the closure of virtually all theatres in Britain, and the dismantling of the Globe and Blackfriars. Performances were thenceforth illicit and rare, staged in private rooms or covered tennis courts, the rectangular shape of which, together with the masque tradition, clearly influenced the design prevalent in the second generation of theatre-building in Britain.

This resurgence began with the Restoration of the monarchy in 1660. In the following year the renewed acceptability of drama was confirmed when a real tennis court was converted into the first Theatre Royal in Drury Lane, Covent Garden where a temporary playhouse had stood in 1636. This had been destroyed by fire and its successor, which opened in 1674, was the first purpose-built post-Elizabethan playhouse in Britain. The architect was Sir Christopher Wren who introduced an important innovation — the fan-shaped auditorium with its side walls sloping inwards towards the stage, so as to continue the illusion of perspective represented behind it. Wren's theatre also contained provision for scenery behind the stage. With a proscenium arch, wings, and pit area seating, it came very close in design to modern theatres — except for retaining the projecting apron stage on which actors were used to performing. The Theatre Royal was remodelled more than once, and was completely rebuilt in 1812, following another fire, to the design of Benjamin Wyatt; over the next twenty years a portico and colonnade were added. The present auditorium dates from 1922, when it was designed by the firm of Emblin, Walker, Jones and Cromie. The site is the oldest continuously occupied theatrical location in Britain.

The oldest theatre building still in regular use is the Theatre Royal, Bristol which opened in 1766 on a site in King Street next to the then recently completed new hall of the city's Company of Coopers (barrel-makers). The architect, Thomas Patey, made a careful study of the 1674 Drury Lane Theatre but introduced significant differences: his auditorium is an elongated semicircle and there was originally no third (gallery)level. The main King Street elevation

Plate 48 The Georgian Theatre Royal, Bristol, with the contemporary Coopers' Hall as its new front entrance. *(Bristol Old Vic Trust)*

was surprisingly modest — a plain gabled Georgian front with a later porch — but the building drew praise as a theatre; the actor and manager David Garrick called it 'the most complete of its dimensions in Europe'.

The Theatre Royal has been extensively altered on several occasions. The auditorium was enlarged in 1800 by the then manager John Palmer (see page 123, Post Offices) and most of its internal decoration was added during the early nineteenth century. In 1972 a further remodelling by Peter Moro and Partners produced a new stage and backstage area and opened up the renovated Coopers' Hall (now owned by Bristol City Council) as the theatre's new foyer — one considerably grander than the previous entrance which has been demolished and replaced by a studio theatre with offices above in modern design. It is a happy accident of architectural history that the hall, with its Palladian-style façade designed by William Halfpenny, survived for nearly two centuries after the declining Coopers' Company had relinquished possession, and has provided so fitting a public face for the theatre.

Because of the alterations undergone by the Theatre Royal, the claim to be the oldest authentic period survival belongs to the Georgian Theatre Royal at Richmond, north Yorkshire, designed in 1788 by an unknown architect and built in three months for the actor manager Samuel Butler. It was closed in 1841 and served as an auction room and wine store until it was rediscovered a century later; it was finally reopened in 1963 after restoration by the architect Richard Leacroft and the theatre historian Dr Richard Southern. Now listed Grade I, it is a rectangular Georgian box only 24.7 by 8.5m (81 by 28ft) in area; its exterior is no more elevated in architecture than the stone barns of its surrounding countryside. The interior is completely original, with bench seating in the pit surrounded on three sides by a tier of boxes and a gallery supported on timber Tuscan arches; it was built for an audience of 450.

THE GLOBE RESTORED

The history of theatre architecture in Britain is coming full circle in more senses than one. Near to the original site in Southwark, work began in 1988 on a reconstruction of Shakespeare's Globe Theatre, with the intention of making it as close as possible to the original as a permanent working monument to the world's greatest playwright. The £18 million project was inspired by the American actor and director Sam Wanamaker who conceived the idea of creating a new 'Wooden O', built as Shakespeare described the original in the preface to *Henry V*:

> . . . But pardon, gentles all,
> The flat unraised spirits that hath dar'd
> On this unworthy scaffold to bring forth

Plate 49 The Bow Street entrance of the Royal Opera House, Covent Garden. *(Royal Opera House, Covent Garden)*

> So great an object: can this cockpit hold
> The vasty fields of France? or may we cram
> Within this Wooden O the very casques
> That did affright the air at Agincourt? . . .
> Suppose within the girdle of these walls
> Are now confin'd two mighty monarchies . . .

The original Globe was typical of its time: a polygonal, oak-framed building, with walls of wattle and daub, and three tiers of covered seating around an unroofed stage which projected into a yard, with standing room for the groundlings. The present-day architects Pentagram have designed a faithful reconstruction, except that the roof will be tiled instead of covered with thatch — it was thatch which led to the destruction of the original when sparks from a cannon set light to it during a performance of *Henry VIII*. When completed it will be an international shrine for theatre lovers.

The theatres described in this chapter represent, from the historical point of view, the most significant of the thousands which once flourished. There are fewer than a hundred still in use in the British Isles; in 1914, there were over 1,000.

OPERA HOUSES

The Royal Opera House in London's Covent Garden occupies a site which has been dedicated to the theatre since 1732, when Edward Shepherd built the Covent Garden Theatre — this was situated off the piazza laid out in 1631–7 to the designs of Inigo Jones (see page 92, Markets). After more than one rebuilding it burned down in 1808 and was replaced the following year by a new theatre designed by Sir Robert Smirke; this was London's first building in the pure Doric style of the Greek Revival, of which Smirke was a leading proponent (see page 97, Museums). In 1847 the theatre was remodelled as an opera house by Benedict Albano, but this burned down again in 1856, It was finally replaced by the present building, designed by E. M. Barry and which opened in 1858; it remains the oldest intact theatrical building still in use in London and the oldest opera house in Britain. It is currently the headquarters of the Royal Opera and the Royal Ballet. Barry's building was followed over the next half century by opera houses in Wakefield (1894), Belfast (1895), Harrogate and Dunfermline (1900), Buxton (1903) and Manchester (1912). Those in Belfast, Buxton and Harrogate have recently been restored.

In 1974, the Covent Garden produce market which had traded in the area since the mid-seventeenth century moved to new premises in south London. Its departure created the opportunity for a major development scheme designed to provide a larger, more modern and efficient stage for the Royal Opera House, better accommodation for the Royal Opera and Royal Ballet companies, and a new public entrance from Covent Garden. An international architectural competition resulted in the appointment of Jeremy Dixon, working in conjunction with Building Design Partnership, as designers for the Royal Opera House development.

ZOOS

Collecting animals was, like amassing works of art and natural curiosities, originally the private pursuit of the princely and powerful who maintained menageries of exotic creatures for their personal amusement and as evidence of their wealth and power. In the twelfth century Henry I kept lions, lynxes, leopards and camels at his country palace at Woodstock, near Oxford, and his grandson Henry II made the Woodstock collection the nucleus of a larger and permanent royal menagerie at the Tower of London, augmented by gifts from other European monarchs. Among new arrivals were a polar bear, the gift of the King of Norway, which was taken down to the Thames each night to fish for its supper; and the first elephant ever seen in Britain.

The Tower menagerie was at first established on a riverside wharf and then later moved into the semicircular Lion Tower, built originally by Edward I as a barbican (watch tower) on the outer side of the Tower moat. The animals were kept in tiers of cages, or 'grates' as the seventeenth-century diarist John Evelyn described them, in conditions which became grossly inadequate — by the eighteenth century, visitors were being offered the choice of paying an admission fee or bringing a cat or dog to be thrown live to the beasts. The animals' treatment was no better in the commercially run menageries in towns, descendants of the travelling shows which had been regular attractions at fairs since the later Middle Ages.

The best known of these ventures was at Exeter 'Change, a commercial development off the Strand built in imitation of the Royal Exchange (see page 44, Exchanges) which had a shopping bazaar on the ground floor. In 1826 the 'Change's elephant went berserk and had to be shot; two years later the whole menagerie moved out, first to the Royal Mews at Charing Cross (where the National Gallery now stands — see page 99, Museums) and then in 1830 to the grounds of Walworth Manor where its proprietor established the Surrey Zoological Gardens, the centrepiece of which was a large conservatory containing lions' and tigers' cages and surrounded by an aviary. The Gardens closed in 1856 in the face of competition from the world's first planned zoo, by then well established in Regent's Park.

London Zoo was the inspiration of Sir Stamford Raffles, who had risen through the East India Company (see page 103, Offices) to become the founder of the Port of Singapore. An enthusiastic natural historian, he chaired the first meeting of the Zoological Society which convened in 1826 to found an institution designed for the scientific care and study of exotic animals, which would replace the previous haphazard collections and menageries assembled merely as spectacles.

Levels of interest and of financial support were both encouraging, and progress was rapid; within months the society had identified a suitable site in Regent's Park, north-west London and had secured a lease from the Crown Estate.

Raffles took as his model an ambitious, but unrealised, plan for the development of the Jardin des Plantes in Paris which he had visited in 1817 after the Napoleonic Wars. Founded in 1626 as a botanical garden by Louis XIII, the Jardin had acquired its first animals in 1794, the survivors of the ransacking of the menagerie at the Palace of Versailles during the French Revolution. It subsequently extended its collection thanks to donations by Napoleon. In 1800 the Jardin's architect, M Verniquet, proposed landscaping the grounds with a variety of terrains and habitats — without success in his own case. To lay out the site and design the first buildings the society therefore called in Decimus Burton, a young architect who had made a name for himself with his work in the royal parks and at Kew Gardens. By 1827 he had produced outline plans for the site, and later that year the zoo opened to members of the Zoological Society. Non-members were first admitted in 1828, but only on payment of an entrance fee and production of a ticket supplied by a member — exclusivity was the original intention. At this stage, the zoo had no permanent buildings, only paddocks and aviaries.

Despite Burton's appointment as the zoo's official architect in 1830 few of his plans were realised, for financial and political reasons. His surviving works include the llama house of 1828 (later the camel house); the giraffe house (1836) — for whose occupants a special expedition penetrated deep into the Sudan; an

Plate 50 The camel house at London Zoo, from an 1835 drawing by George Scharf. *(Zoological Society of London)*

aviary; and he also designed the old tunnel with its classical entrances, built in 1830 to link the two original areas of zoo grounds which were separated by the Outer Circle, the carriage road running round the inside perimeter of the park. The camel house (with its later clock tower) and the giraffe house (subsequently modified) are simple, workmanlike structures which convey the informality of the early days of the zoo, when it first began to grow with the aid of donations and acquisitions of animals of special interest. By 1831 William IV had handed over the royal menageries — one housed in the Tower and a later collection in Windsor Great Park — and the society was being offered animals from all over the world, which needed to be housed. During the remainder of the nineteenth century the London Zoo maintained its pioneering role with the building of the first reptile (now bird) house of 1849, the first public aquarium (1853) and the first insect house (1881). By this time three more zoos, inspired by the success of London, had opened in the British Isles — Dublin (1831), Bristol (1835) and Manchester (1836).

With the twentieth century came a new approach to the display of animals — naturalism. Based on the principles of the German zoologist Carl Hagenbeck, this meant creating 'bar-less' panoramas, with minimal evidence of restraint and in which animals were allowed as much freedom of movement as was compatible with the space available and with the safety of other species (including the human race). He put his thinking into practice in the Tiergarten at Hamburg, opened in 1907, where he built rocky vistas of concrete on wooden and metal supports with the animals' caves below and deep ditches as the safety barrier between them and the public. The Tiergarten inspired the Royal Zoological Society of Scotland which was founded two years later, and which opened Edinburgh Zoo in the Corstophine Hill House estate in 1913; it also inspired a new outlook at Regent's Park where it found expression in the creation of the Mappin Terraces for London's polar bears. The Terraces were the idea of Chalmers Mitchell, the secretary of London Zoo, who became an enthusiast of the Hagenbeck approach after a European tour. He secured the financial support of the jeweller J. Newton Mappin who agreed to contribute 'an installation for the panoramic display of wild animals'; designed by John Belcher and his partner John James Joass, the Terraces opened in 1913 with the space beneath allocated to a new aquarium which opened in 1924. In 1989 the zoo announced plans for remodelling the Terraces as part of a £10 million government-funded development plan.

In the 1930s London Zoo was again at the forefront of zoological thinking, as it was responsible for the opening of the world's first country zoo at Whipsnade in Bedfordshire. The idea of Regent's Park opening a rural satellite, originally for the recuperation of sick animals, had first been considered in 1903, and in 1921 the society had seriously contemplated Crystal Palace (see page 52, Exhibition centres). By this time the zoo's 14ha (36 acre) site in Regent's Park was being intensively used, but the Crown Estate commissioners were proving unreceptive to suggestions of further encroachment southwards into the park, which was the most convenient direction to move in. The society therefore decided to purchase a country property and acquired Hall Farm at Whipsnade where its 194ha

(480 acre) park opened in 1931. Both zoos have their own collections and also regularly exchange animals.

Whipsnade is the immediate ancestor of the wildlife and safari parks, which have developed the Hagenbeck approach to the extent of having animals roaming at large in open parkland; visitors are no longer static spectators, but can drive through the park. This particular scene was set at Longleat in Wiltshire, where the first nature reserve for lions in the western world was established in 1966 by the Marquis of Bath, owner of the Longleat estate, and Jimmy Chipperfield of the circus family.

From a mere four zoos in the nineteenth century the number of zoos, wildlife and safari parks, bird sanctuaries, aquaria and dolphinaria, and children's zoos in the British Isles has risen to well over a hundred. Among them are Belfast Zoo, Northern Ireland, the first to be set up (in 1933) by a local authority; and Dudley, which occupies the grounds of a medieval castle.

BUILDINGS AND SITES OF PARTICULAR INTEREST

Entries are by county or (in Scotland) region (in bold) and then city, town or district (in italic), with counties and regions reflecting the reorganisations of Greater London (1965), England and Wales (1974), Northern Ireland (1973) and Scotland (1975). Please note that Greater London, Greater Manchester, Merseyside, Tyne & Wear and West Yorkshire are retained as convenient geographical descriptions despite the abolition of the metropolitan counties of those names in 1986.

ENGLAND

Avon

Bristol

Rummer Inn, All Saints Lane, Bristol 1. Rebuilt in Georgian period on site of the city's oldest inn, the Rummer Inn was the Bristol end of first mail coach run, 1784.

Theatre Royal, King Street, Bristol 1. Oldest theatre building still in regular use, opened 1766.

Bedfordshire

South Bedfordshire

Whipsnade Park, Dunstable, Bedfordshire. (Access from M1 junction 9, then A5; or junction 11, then A505). The world's first country zoo, opened in 1931.

Berkshire

Windsor & Maidenhead

Windsor Castle. Oldest building in the world in continuous use as a royal home; original citadel of 1080 rebuilt in twelfth and later centuries.

Buckinghamshire

Milton Keynes

The Point, Midsummer Boulevard, Central Milton Keynes. Leisure centre containing Britain's first purpose-built multiplex cinema, opened 1985.

Cleveland

Stockton

Billingham Forum, The Causeway, Billingham, Cleveland. Opened 1967; first leisure complex in Britain containing theatre as well as sports halls.

Cornwall

Kerrier

Goonhilly Earth Satellite Station, Goonhilly Downs, near Helston (off B3293 Helston-Coverack Road). Britain's first earth satellite station, completed 1962.

Cumbria

Copeland

Calder Hall Nuclear Power Station, Sellafield, Seascale (off A595 between Ravenglass and Whitehaven). Earliest industrial-scale nuclear power station in the world, commissioned 1956.

Whitehaven (historic town centre), (on A595 between Barrow and Carlisle). Earliest planned industrial town in Britain, founded 1660s.

Derbyshire

Derby

Midland Hotel, Midland Road. Earliest surviving purpose-built railway hotel, opened 1840.

Silk Mill (now Derby Industrial Museum), off Full Street. First purpose-built power-driven factory in Britain; built early eighteenth century, rebuilt 1910.

Devon
Plymouth
Bronze Age port settlement, Mount Batten, Plymstock. Earliest international port discovered in Britain, 900–800BC.

Royal Naval Hospital, Stonehouse. First hospital planned on pavilion principle, completed 1765.

Dorset
West Dorset
Maiden Castle (off A354 south of Dorchester). Well-preserved survival of Celtic hill fortification.

East Sussex
Hastings
Hastings Castle. Ruins of stone fortification rebuilt on site of first post-Conquest Norman castle of 1066.

Essex
Colchester
Roman site, Butt Road (adjacent to police station). Earliest Roman church excavated in Britain, dated to 320.

Harlow
Harlow Sportcentre, Hammarskjold Road. First community sports complex, opened 1964.

Harwich
Electric Palace cinema, King's Quay Street. Oldest substantially unaltered cinema in Britain still giving public performances, built 1911.

Greater London
Barnet
Brent Cross Shopping Centre, Hendon Way, NW4. First out-of-town shopping centre in Britain, opened 1976.

Bromley
Crystal Palace Exhibition Centre, Crystal Palace Park, SE19 (site). Britain's first purpose-designed international exhibition building, originally erected in Hyde Park 1851, moved here in 1854, destroyed by fire 1936.

Camden
British Library (new), Euston Road, NW1. Work began 1982 on replacement for British Museum Reading Room (see below).

British Museum, Great Russell Street, WC1. First purpose-designed home for national collections, completed 1857. Reading Room (started 1854) was the first purpose-built home of Britain's national library collection.

Euston Station, Euston Square, NW1. London's first main-line railway terminus, opened 1837.

King's Cross Station, Euston Road, N1. Oldest substantially unaltered London rail terminus.

St Etheldreda's Church, Ely Place, EC1. Oldest church in use for Catholic worship, dating from c1290.

City
Bank of England, Threadneedle Street, EC2. First purpose-built premises completed in 1734; part of Soane's rebuilding (post-1788) was re-created in an on-site museum, opened 1988.

Fountain House, Fenchurch Street, EC3. First high-rise commercial office tower in London, developed 1957.

Guildhall, Guildhall Yard, EC2. Oldest continuously used civic building in Britain, built 1411–40 on site of twelfth-century predecessor.

Hoare's Bank, Fleet Street, EC4. Last surviving private deposit bank. Present building completed 1832.

King Edward Building, King Edward Street, EC1. Only survivor of complex of Post Office headquarter buildings around St Martin's-le-Grand; still in postal use.

Lloyd's Building, Leadenhall Street, EC3. Completed in 1986 on site of East India House, in turn the earliest purpose-designed building for a trading organisation, completed 1729.

Museum of London, London Wall, EC2. First purpose-designed interpretative museum, opened 1976.

Royal Exchange, EC3. Successor, completed 1844, of first specialised commercial building in Britain, opened 1568.

St Bartholomew's Hospital, West Smithfield, EC1. Oldest established hospital still occupying original site; founded 1123, rebuilt mid-eighteenth century.

Spanish and Portuguese Jews' Congregation, Bevis Marks, EC3. Oldest synagogue in Britain, opened 1701.

Croydon/Sutton
Airport House (former Croydon Airport Terminal), Purley Way, South Croydon. Croydon was Britain's first official civil airport, opened 1920. World's first purpose-built air terminal built here 1928, closed 1959; now business premises.

Greenwich
Deptford Power Station (site), The Stowage, SE8. First purpose-designed power station in Britain, commissioned 1889.

Haringey
Alexandra Palace, Wood Green, N22. Opened as entertainment centre 1873.

Home of first regular television service in world, inaugurated 1936.

Hillingdon
Heathrow Airport, Bath Road, (access via M4/A4). Used as airport 1919–20 and from 1946; earliest permanent terminal opened 1955. Runway covers London end of world's first regular scheduled international air service, inaugurated 1919.

Islington
Farringdon (Metropolitan Line) Station, Cowcross Street, EC1. Eastern terminus of world's first underground railway, opened 1863.

Pentonville Prison, Caledonian Road, N7. Prototype of modern prison, completed 1842.

Kensington and Chelsea
Electric Cinema, Portobello Road, W11. Oldest extant purpose-built cinema in Britain (closed in 1987).

Lambeth
Bon Marché, Brixton Road, SW9. First department store planned as such from outset, 1877.

Kennington (Northern Line) Station, Kennington Park Road, SE11. Surviving surface-level station building of world's first deep-level tube railway.

Southwark
Dulwich Picture Gallery, College Road, SE21. Earliest independent public art gallery, completed 1814.

Elephant and Castle Shopping Centre, SE1. Earliest modern shopping centre built on arcade principle, opened 1965.

Globe Theatre site, Bankside, SE1. 1598 original built with timber from Britain's first recorded permanent theatre (1576). Building work on reconstruction began 1988.

London Bridge Station, SE1. Site of

first permanent railway terminus in London, opened 1836.

Tower Hamlets

Brunswick Dock (later East India Docks), East India Dock Road, E14. First enclosed dock in Britain, built c1660 for ship building and repair.

St Katharine Dock, St Katharine's Way, E1. Earliest commercial dock built complete with warehouses, 1828.

Tower of London, Tower Hill, EC3. Britain's oldest castle still in military use, on site of Norman timber fortification of 1067. White Tower earliest of present buildings, completed c1098. Armouries first opened to public 1670.

Westminster

Banqueting Hall, Whitehall, SW1. Earliest surviving building designed for theatrical use, completed 1622.

Broadcasting House, Portland Place, W1. First purpose-built broadcasting complex in Britain, operational 1932.

Buckingham Palace, The Mall, SW1. Main royal residence, core dating from 1702.

Covent Garden Market, WC2. Oldest surviving nineteenth-century market building hall, opened in stages from 1829.

Empire Cinema, (formerly 'Empire Music Hall'), Leicester Square, WC2. Venue of first regular public film shows in Britain, 1896.

Great Western Royal Hotel, Praed Street, Paddington Station, W2. Earliest surviving railway hotel in London.

Horse Guards, Whitehall, SW1. Oldest barracks site in Britain, present building completed 1759.

Houses of Parliament, Palace of Westminster, SW1. Begun in 1840 on site of the Palace of Westminster, used for meetings of Commons as well as Lords from 1325.

Institution of Electrical Engineers, Savoy Place, WC2. Home of first corporate BBC headquarters 1923, at no 2 Savoy Hill (west wing of Savoy Place).

Jewel Tower, Old Palace Yard, SW1. Oldest unaltered Government building in Britain, completed 1366.

London Zoo, Regent's Park, NW1. World's first planned zoological gardens, opened 1827.

National Gallery, Trafalgar Square, WC2. First purpose-built home for national art collections, opened 1838.

Paddington (District Line) Underground Station, Praed Street, W2. Western terminus of world's first underground railway, opened 1863.

Queen's Chapel, Marlborough Gate, SW1. Earliest post-Reformation church built for Catholic worship, completed 1625; now Church of England.

Royal Opera Arcade, Pall Mall, SW1. First shopping arcade in Britain, opened 1817.

Royal Opera House, Bow Street, WC2. Oldest opera house in Britain, present building dates from 1858.

Selfridges, Oxford Street, W1. First West End department store to open in own buildings, 1909.

Simpson's Restaurant, The Strand, WC2. Earliest modern restaurant, opened 1828, rebuilt 1848 and replaced 1904 by present building.

Somerset House, The Strand, WC2. First purpose-built government office complex in Britain, completed 1800.

Theatre Royal, Drury Lane. Oldest still-used theatrical site in Britain, in use since seventeenth century.

Westminster Hall, Palace of Westminster, SW1. Oldest extant government building in Britain, dating in original form from 1099.

Greater Manchester
Manchester
Chetham's Library, Hunt's Bank, Manchester 3. Oldest free public library still in original buildings, opened 1655.

Granada TV Centre, Quay Street, Manchester 3. First purpose-designed television station in Britain, operational 1956; original studio still in use.

Kendals, Deansgate, Manchester 3. Oldest department store in Britain; originated as drapers 1796, first purpose-built premises 1831.

Liverpool Road Station (now Greater Manchester Museum of Science and Industry), Liverpool Road, Castlefield, Manchester 3. Earliest purpose-built passenger railway station, opened 1830.

Trafford
Trafford Park Industrial Estate, Trafford Park Road, Manchester 17. 'Mother of industrial estates', began 1896.

Hampshire
Winchester
Habel's Store (formerly County Gaol, then Library), Jewry Street. First rate-supported public library in Britain, opened 1851.

Winchester College. Earliest school to be planned and built as an educational institution, established 1382; the original schoolroom, dating from 1394, survives as a study room.

Kent
Canterbury
Canterbury Cathedral. Original foundation of St Augustine destroyed by fire in 1067; rebuilt 1070–7. Earliest surviving monastic hospital building in Britain dates from twelfth century.

King's School, The Precincts. Founded 598 as an annexe of Canterbury Cathedral.

St Martin's Church, St Martin's Hill. Oldest Christian church continuously in use; of Roman origin and/or materials, recorded as being used for Christian worship by 570 and probably extended by St Augustine in AD 597.

Merseyside
Liverpool
Albert Dock, Liverpool 3. Part of first planned commercial enclosed dock system in Britain, started 1710. Albert Dock warehouses, the country's largest concentration of Grade I listed buildings, are now a shopping and entertainment centre.

St John's Market (site redeveloped as St John's Centre), Liverpool 1. First major covered market hall in Britain; completed 1822, demolished 1964.

William Brown Library, William Brown Street, Liverpool 1. First major purpose-designed library building in Britain, opened 1860.

North Yorkshire
Richmond
Georgian Theatre Royal, Victoria Road, Richmond. Oldest unaltered theatre in Britain, opened 1788.

York
St Peter's Hospital, Museum Street (site). Earliest recorded hospital building in Britain, foundation traditionally dated to 937.

Oxfordshire
Oxford
Congregation House, St Mary the Virgin, High Street. Earliest university building in Britain, dating from early fourteenth century. Room above is the oldest surviving library building in Britain, built around 1320; now used as a parish room.

Merton College, Merton Street. Oldest collegiate university buildings in Britain, college founded 1264.

Museum of the History of Science, Old Ashmolean Building, Broad Street. First purpose-designed public museum, opened 1683.

New College, New College Lane. First college planned and built as a unity, begun 1380. The library was the first to have been built integrally with the college, completed by 1386.

Surrey
Woking
Shah Jehan Mosque, Oriental Road. Earliest mosque in Britain, completed 1890.

Tyne & Wear
Gateshead
Metrocentre (off A69 Gateshead Western Bypass). First British shopping centre with 'leisure box', opened 1988.

Warwickshire
Stratford-upon-Avon
Pedagogue's House (King Edward VI School), off Church Street. Oldest distinct school building still in educational use, completed 1427.

West Midlands
Birmingham
Bingley Hall Exhibition Centre (former), Broad Street, Birmingham 1 (site redeveloped as Birmingham Convention Centre). First purpose-built exhibition centre, opened 1850.

Bull Ring Centre, Smallbrook Queensway, Birmingham 5. First modern enclosed shopping centre, opened 1964.

Solihull
National Exhibition Centre, Bickenhill, Birmingham 40 (access from M6). Opened in 1976.

West Sussex
Crawley
'Beehive' building, Gatwick Airport. Oldest surviving British airport building still in operational use, completed 1936.

West Yorkshire
Leeds
Town Hall, Victoria Square. Earliest town hall with administrative offices, completed 1858.

Wiltshire
Kennet
Avebury Ring (near intersection of A4 and A361, west of Marlborough). Early stone circles, dated to 3500BC.

West Wiltshire
Longleat Safari Park, Longleat, Warminster (off A362 between Warminster and Frome). First nature reserve with lions in western world, opened 1966.

WALES
South Glamorgan
Cardiff
Cardiff Civic Centre, Cathays Park. Earliest civic centre complex; planning began 1899.

SCOTLAND
Dumfries and Galloway Region
Nithsdale
Sanquhar Post Office, High Street, Sanquhar. Oldest post office in Britain, in continuous use since 1800.

Wigtown
Whithorn ecclesiastical sites, Whithorn (reached by A714/A746

from Newton Stewart). Ruins of church built fifth century AD by St Ninian, first Scottish bishop; part of cluster of buildings used successively for Christian worship for some 1,600 years.

Lothian Region
Edinburgh
Holyrood House Palace, Canongate. Oldest royal residence in Scotland, originally founded as an abbey, 1128.

Parliament House, Parliament Square. Completed in 1640, the first purpose-built parliament building in Britain is now used as an assembly hall for courts.

Strathclyde Region
Argyll and Bute
Iona ecclesiastical sites, Island of Iona, off Island of Mull (reached by A849 after ferry from Oban). Site of St Columba's missionary centre, dated around 563.

Glasgow
St Enoch (Underground) Station, St Enoch Square, Glasgow 1. Surviving original station on Britain's first underground railway built in a single operation.

Lanark
Leadhills Library, Biggar. First independent subscription library in Britain, 1741.

NORTHERN IRELAND
Belfast
Belfast Zoo, Bellevue, Antrim Road. First zoo in Britain established by a local authority, 1933.

SOUTHERN IRELAND
Dublin
Bank of Ireland (formerly Irish Parliament House), College Green. Irish Parliament met here for the first time in 1731; its design inspired that of the British Museum.

Royal (later Collins) Barracks, Benburb Street. Oldest surviving barracks in British Isles, completed 1709.

ISLE OF MAN
St John's
Tynwald Hill. Oldest parliamentary site in British Isles, established by Vikings who began settling on the island during the ninth century.

NOTES ON ARCHITECTS,
ENGINEERS AND MASONS

Abraham, Robert (1774–1850). Building Surveyor and later architect. Designer of the County Fire Office, Regent Street (1819).

Air Ministry Architect's Department. Designers of Croydon Airport Terminal (1928).

Avis, Joseph (late seventeenth century). A tailor by trade, he built the Bevis Marks Synagogue, opened 1701.

Bage, Charles (1752–1822). Designer of the Benyon flax mill at Shrewsbury (1797).

Baker, Sir Benjamin (1840–1907). A Victorian railway engineer, he worked with Sir John Fowler (qv) on London's Metropolitan Railway (1863) and later as Fowler's partner on the City and South London Railway (1890).

Barry, Sir Charles (1795–1860). Leading early Victorian architect in practice in London from 1820. In 1835 he won the competition for the new Houses of Parliament (begun 1840), on which he worked with Augustus Welby Pugin.

Barry, Edward Middleton (1830–80). Son of Sir Charles Barry (qv). Architect of the present Royal Opera House, Covent Garden (1858).

Belcher, John (1841–1913) and **Joass, John James (1868–1952).** Designers of the Mappin Terraces at London Zoo (1913).

Bernard Engle Partnership (formed originally in 1850). Architects of Brent Cross Shopping Centre (1976).

Blomfield, Sir Reginald (1856–1942). Edwardian architect and consultant on the design of pylons for the National Grid.

Boissevain & Osmond (formed 1961). Competition-winning architects of the Elephant and Castle Shopping Centre in south London (1965).

Brodrick, Cuthbert (1822–1905). Yorkshire architect who worked mainly in Leeds. His Leeds Town Hall (1858) is one of the best classical buildings in the country.

Building Design Partnership (formed 1961). Architects, jointly with interior designer Neil Tibbatts, of The Point Leisure Centre and Multiplex Cinema at Milton Keynes (1985).

Burgh, Lt-Col Thomas (1670–1730). Chief Engineer of Ireland from 1700 to his death, he designed the Royal (now Collins) Barracks in Dublin (1701–9).

Burton, Decimus (1800–81). Active by the age of twenty-four, he won important commissions in the royal parks before setting up in private practice. He produced the original plan for the London Zoo in Regent's Park (1827) and designed its earliest buildings.

Chambers, Sir William (1723–96). Set up in practice in London in 1755 and became architectural tutor to George III. In 1761 he joined the Office of Works, becoming its Controller in 1769. As Britain's chief official architect he designed Somerset House (completed in 1800 after his death).

Chambers, W. I. (late nineteenth century). Designer of the Shah Jehan Mosque in Woking, Surrey.

Chatwin, Julius (1830–1907). As a pupil of Charles Barry he worked on drawings for the new Houses of Parliament. Later, in practice on his own account in Birmingham, he designed Bingley Hall (1850).

Croxton, John (1411–47). A London master mason, he spent over thirty years of his life working on the buildings of the City of London, among them the Guildhall (1411–40).

Cubitt, Lewis (1799–1883). Brother of the builders Thomas and William Cubitt for whom he designed many of his buildings. Architect of King's Cross Station, the oldest surviving intact London railway terminus, with his brother Joseph, the engineer to the Great Northern Railway and their father Sir William as consultant.

de Ferranti, Sebastian (1864–1930). Electrical engineer. Designer of the machinery, electrical equipment and buildings at Deptford Power Station (1889).

de Yevele, Henry (c1320–1400). Appointed King's Master Mason in 1365, he remodelled Westminster Hall (1395–1402) and designed and built the Jewel Tower (completed 1366).

Elder Lester and Partners (formed 1955). Architects of Billingham Forum leisure complex, opened 1967.

Figgis, Thomas Phillips (1858–1948). Architect of station buildings for the City and South London Railway (1890).

Foster, John Jr (c1786–1846). Architect and surveyor to Liverpool Corporation 1824–35 in succession to his father, he designed a number of important buildings in the city (of which few survive) including the now-demolished St John's Market (1822).

Fowler, Charles (1791–1867). Born in Devon, he set up in practice in London in 1818. Architect of the Covent Garden Market building (1829).

Fowler, Sir John (1817–98). A railway engineer, he designed the Metropolitan Railway and its stations (1863). Later he was joint consulting engineer with Sir Benjamin Baker (qv) on the City and South London Railway (1890).

Gibberd, Sir Frederick (1908–84). Founder of Frederick Gibberd and Partners. Architect of the Harlow Sportcentre, Essex (1964), the first permanent terminal buildings at London Heathrow Airport (1955) and the Regent's Park Mosque (1978).

Gibbs, James (1682–1754). Trained professionally in Italy, he set up in practice in 1709. Designed the new buildings of St Bartholomew's Hospital (1730 onwards).

Greenwood, Sidney (1908–72). Chief architect to the Laing group from 1947, he designed the Bull Ring Centre at Birmingham (1964).

Gundulf (c1022–1108). A Norman abbot who became Bishop of Rochester in 1077, he was an expert in castle construction and was appointed by William the Conqueror to supervise the first permanent buildings at the Tower of London from 1081.

Haigh, Thomas (early nineteenth century). A probable candidate as architect of Liverpool Road Station, Manchester (1830), he was a partner in the Liverpool firm of Haigh and Franklin.

Hardwick, Philip (1792–1870). Son of Thomas Hardwick (qv). Architect with Thomas Telford (qv) of the St Katharine Dock warehouses (1828) and of the entrance portico and railway hotels at Euston Station (1840); with his son Philip C. Hardwick (1820–90) he later designed the Great Hall at Euston.

Hardwick, Thomas (1752–1829). Pupil of Sir William Chambers. Architect with William Wilkins (qv) of the Millbank Penitentiary (1811–21).

Hooper, Harold Ridley (1885–1953). East Anglian-based architect who began practice on his own account in 1911 with the Electric Palace at Harwich (1911).

Husband and Co (formed 1936). Designers of the first earth-satellite station at Goonhilly, Cornwall (1962).

Jacobsen, Theodore (d1772). Descendant of a German family of Hanseatic merchants, he ran a successful London business and became an amateur architect. Designer (with John James, a professional surveyor) of the offices of the East India Company in Leadenhall Street (1729).

Jebb, Sir Joshua (1793–1863). A military engineer by training, he was appointed Surveyor-General of Prisons in 1837 to advise the government on the design and construction of prisons, and was responsible for the new model prison at Pentonville, north London (1842). He published the manual *Modern Prisons: their Construction and Ventilation* in 1844.

Jones, Inigo (1573–1652). Theatrical designer and architect who introduced the Palladian style of classical architecture into Britain. Architect of the Banqueting House, Whitehall (1622), the Queen's Chapel in Marlborough Gate (1625) and the Covent Garden Piazza (1637).

Kent, William (1685–1748). Painter, official architect and landscape gardener. Designer of the present Horse Guards in Whitehall (1759) which was completed after his death.

Lamb, Thomas W. (1871–1942). Scottish born, he became America's first and most prolific cinema architect. Working with the office of Frank Matcham (1854–1920), he converted the Empire Theatre, Leicester Square into a 3,500-seater cinema.

L. G. Mouchel and Partners (formed 1897). Civil engineering consultants. Designers of Britain's first hyperbolic concrete cooling towers at Liverpool (1925).

London County Council's Department of Architecture and Civic Design (architect **Sir Leslie Martin,** then **Sir Hubert Bennett**). Designers of the National Recreation Centre at Crystal Palace (opened 1964).

Marlow, Alan (b1907). Principal partner in the partnership of Hoar, Marlow & Lovett, formed specially to design the circular 'beehive' terminal at Gatwick Airport (1936).

Murray, Sir James (d1634). Scottish architect who succeeded his father James Murray Sr as Overseer of the King's Works in Scotland in 1605. Designer of the Parliament Hall in Edinburgh (1640).

Myer, Lt-Col George Val (1883–1959). A pupil of John Belcher (qv), he was the architect of Broadcasting House (1932).

Nash, John (1752–1835). Favourite architect of the Prince Regent (later George IV), his greatest achievement was the replanning of the West End of London, including the creation of Regent's Park on the site of Marylebone Farm and its linking by a grand processional route (Portland Place and Regent Street) to the royal domain of St James. Working with George Repton (1786–1858), he designed the Royal Opera Arcade as the approach to an early opera house.

Parker, Charles (1799–1881). Italian-trained architect whose researches were a prime source for early Victorian Italianate architecture. Designer of Hoare's Bank in Fleet Street (1832).

Parsons and Rawlings: formed by **Henry Parsons, 1828/9–1902.** Architects of Bon Marché in Brixton, south London (1877).

Patey, Thomas (1712/13–89). Member of a prolific Bristol family of masons and architects. Designer of the Theatre Royal, Bristol (1766).

Paxton, Sir Joseph (1801–65). Horticulturalist and structural pioneer. Designed the Crystal Palace (1851) using technology which he developed in constructing greenhouses.

Pentagram (formed 1972). Architects of the reconstructed Globe Theatre in Southwark, south London (work began in 1988).

Powell and Moya (formed 1946). Architects of the Museum of London (1976).

Property Services Agency. Designers of Telecom Tower, London (1965).

Pugin, Augustus Welby (1812–52). Designer. Collaborated with Sir Charles Barry (qv) on the new Houses of Parliament (began 1840), for which he produced competition drawings, designed the furniture and fittings, and supervised the interior decoration.

Rahere (late eleventh/early twelfth centuries). Cleric and courtier, designer of the first hospital at St Bartholomew's, London (1123–9).

Repton, George (1786–1855). See under Nash, John.

Ride, William (1749–1775). Architect of the new Horsham County Gaol, 1779, the first to be designed on the cell principle advocated by the prison reform movement, as represented by John Howard.

Rogers, Richard (b1933). Architect of the new Lloyd's Building, Britain's first internally flexible financial exchange.

Rogers, William H. (b1914). Company architect from 1949 of the City of London Real Property Co Ltd (later Land Securities) for whom he designed Fountain House, Fenchurch Street, the first office tower to break the 'jelly-mould' tradition of commercial development.

Rouchead, Alexander (d1776). Designer of the Royal Naval Hospital at Stonehouse, Plymouth, which pioneered the pavilion principle.

Scott, Sir Giles Gilbert (1880–1960). Architect of churches, houses and public buildings. Architect of the rebuilding of the House of Commons and of the City of London Guildhall after bombing in World War II. Architectural Consultant to the building of Battersea Power Station. Designer of range of public telephone boxes which were standard in the UK from 1927 to 1985.

Smirke, Sir Robert (1780–1867). Leading exponent of the Greek Revival. Architect of the Covent Garden Theatre (1809); the first purpose-built headquarters of the General Post Office (1829); and the British Museum (1857).

Smirke, Sydney (1797–1877). Younger brother and pupil of Sir Robert Smirke, he supervised the completion of the British Museum after his brother's retirement from practice in 1846 and designed the domed Reading Room (1857), the first home of the British National Library.

Soane, Sir John (1753–1837). A prolific and influential Georgian architect, he rebuilt the Bank of England (1788–1833), designed the Dulwich Picture Gallery (1811–14) and a pioneering court complex outside Westminster Hall (1826), and turned his own house in Lincoln's Inn Fields into what is now the Soane Museum.

Sorocold, George (b1668). Mechanical and hydraulic engineer. Designer of the prototype modern factories at Derby in the early eighteenth century; adviser to Liverpool Corporation on the construction of the first Liverpool Dock (1710) in conjunction with Thomas Steers (qv).

Steers, Thomas (d1750). Dock engineer to Liverpool Corporation from 1710, he was responsible for the early docks at Liverpool, the first planned commercial dock system in Britain.

Tanner, Sir Henry (1849–1935). Designer of the General Post Office's King Edward Building (1910), one of the earliest official buildings in reinforced concrete construction and the only survivor of the St Martin's-le-Grand complex still in Post Office ownership.

Telford, Thomas (1757–1834). Civil engineer. Designer of the St Katharine dock basin with Philip Hardwick (qv), the first built complete with integral warehouses.

Tite, Sir William (1798–1873). Son of a City of London merchant, later an MP. Architect of the third and present Royal Exchange (1844), the commission for which he won in competition.

Tubbs, Ralph (b1912). Architect of the first purpose-designed TV complex for Granada, Manchester (1956).

van Paesschen, Henryk (sixteenth century). Flemish architect, designer of the first Royal Exchange (completed 1568).

Verity, Thomas (1837–91). Theatre architect. Designed the Empire Theatre, Leicester Square, later the scene of the first public showing of films in Britain, inside the shell of the Royal London Panorama (1888). His son **Frank (d1936)** later remodelled it.

Voysey, Annesley (c1794–1839). Designer of the first block of speculative offices in Clements Lane, City of London (c1823), now demolished.

Wilkins, William (1778–1839). Architect of the National Gallery (1838), the first permanent home of the British national art collection. Together with Thomas Hardwick (qv), he designed the Millbank Penitentiary (1811–21).

Wilson, Colin St John (b1922). Architect of the British Library building, St Pancras, north London (designed 1975; work began on site in 1982).

Wood, Thomas (c1644–95). Master mason, probable designer of the Old Ashmolean Museum, Oxford (1683).

Works, Ministry of (predecessor of Property Services, qv). Designers of Calder Hall nuclear power station.

Wren, Sir Christopher (1632–1732). Britain's greatest architect. Designer of the earliest post-Elizabethan playhouse, the Theatre Royal (1674), and of alterations to the House of Commons after the union of England and Scotland.

Wynford, William (1360–1405). Master mason; builder and probably designer of Winchester College in Hampshire (completed 1394) and New College, Oxford (began 1380) on behalf of William of Wykeham.

BIBLIOGRAPHY

GENERAL

Clark, Sir George (editor). *The Oxford History of England* (Clarendon Press, Oxford, 1936ff)

Colvin, H. M. *A Biographical Dictionary of British Architects 1600–1840* (John Murray, 1978)

Colvin, H.M. (general editor). *History of the King's Works* (HMSO, 1963ff)

Crawford, David. *The City of London: its Architectural Heritage* (Woodhead-Faulkner, Cambridge, 1976)

Dixon, Roger and Muthesius, Stefan. *Victorian Architecture* (Thames & Hudson, 1978)

Gray, A. Stuart. *Edwardian Architecture: a Biographical Dictionary* (Duckworth, 1985)

Hitchcock, Henry-Russell. *Early Victorian Architecture in Britain* (Architectural Press, 1954)

Hobhouse, Hermione. *Lost London* (Macmillan, 1971)

Hunting, Penelope. *Royal Westminster* (Royal Institution of Chartered Surveyors, 1981)

King, Anthony D. (editor). *Buildings and Society* (Routledge & Kegan Paul, 1980)

Pevsner, Nikolaus. *A History of Building Types* (Thames & Hudson, 1976)

Pevsner, Nikolaus and others. *Buildings of England, Buildings of Wales, Buildings of Scotland, Buildings of Ulster* (Penguin Books, 1951ff)

Rolt, L. T. C. *Victorian Engineering* (Penguin Books, 1970)

Rudé, George. *Hanoverian London 1714–1808* (Secker & Warburg, 1971)

Saunders, Ann. *The Art and Architecture of London* (Phaidon, 1988)

Schofield, John. *The Building of London from the Conquest to the Great Fire* (British Museum Publications, 1984)

Sharp, Dennis. *Manchester* (Studio Visto, 1969)

Singer, Charles and others (editors). *A History of Technology* (Oxford University Press, 1963)

Weinreb, Ben and Hibbert, Christopher. *The London Encyclopaedia* (Macmillan, 1983)

AIRPORTS

Chandos, John. *London Airport* (HMSO, 1956)

Harper, Harry and Brenard, Robert. *The Romance of the Flying Mail* (Routledge, 1933)

King, John E. *Gatwick: the Evolution of an Airport* (Gatwick Airport Ltd and Sussex Industrial Archaeology Society, 1986)

BIBLIOGRAPHY

Learmonth, Bob, Nash, Joanna and Cluett, Douglas. *The First Croydon Airport 1915–1928* (Sutton Libraries & Arts Services, 1977)

BROADCASTING BUILDINGS

British Broadcasting Corporation. *Broadcasting House* (BBC, 1932)

Sendall, Bernard. *Independent Television in Britain, volume 1* (Macmillan, 1982)

CINEMAS

Atwell, David. *Cathedrals of the Movies* (Architectural Press, 1980)

High, David. *The First Hundred Years: The Story of the Empire, Leicester Square* (Published by the author, 1985)

Sharp, Dennis. *The Picture Palace* (Hugh Evelyn, 1969)

Strachan, Chris. *The Harwich Electric Palace* (Published by the author, 1979)

CIVIC BUILDINGS

Barron, Caroline M. *The Mediaeval Guildhall of London* (Corporation of London, 1974)

Cunningham, Colin. *Victorian and Edwardian Town Halls* (Routledge & Kegan Paul, 1981)

DEPARTMENT STORES

See page 186, **Shopping Arcades and Malls**

DOCKS

Broodbank, Sir Joseph. *History of the Port of London* (Daniel O'Connor, London, 1921)

Pudney, John. *London's Docks* (Thames & Hudson, 1975)

Ritchie-Noakes, Nancy. *Liverpool's Historic Waterfront* (HMSO, 1984)

EDUCATION BUILDINGS

Catto, J. I. (editor). *The History of the University of Oxford, volume 1* (Oxford University Press, 1984)

Curtis, S. J. *History of Education in Great Britain* (UTP, London, 1950)

Edwards, David L. *A History of King's School, Canterbury* (Faber & Faber 1957)

Fogg, Nicholas. *Stratford-upon-Avon: Portrait of a Town* (Phillimore, 1986)

Green, V. H. H. *The Universities* (Penguin, 1969)

McDonnell, Michael F. J. *A History of St Paul's School* (Chapman & Hall, 1909).

Parker, Keith T. *The Guild Chapel and Other Guild Buildings of Stratford-upon-Avon* (The Guild School Association, Stratford-upon-Avon, 1987)

Seaborne, Malcolm. *The English School* (Routledge & Kegan Paul, 1971)

BIBLIOGRAPHY

EXCHANGES AND FINANCIAL MARKETS

Flower, Raymond and Wynn Jones, Michael. *An Illustrated History of Lloyd's* (Lloyd's, 1981)

See also page 184, **Offices**

EXHIBITION CENTRES

Enefer, Trevor. 'The Great Men and the Gardener who built the Crystal Palace', *The Valuer* (October 1988)

ffrench, Yvonne. *The Great Exhibition 1951* (Harvill Press, 1950)

Granelli, Remo. 'The First National Exhibition', *Architecture West Midlands* (no 24, February/March, 1976)

Hobhouse, Christopher. *1851 and the Crystal Palace* (John Murrary, 1950)

Mills, Edward. *The National Exhibition Centre* (Crosby Lockwood Staples, 1976)

Reeves, Graham. *Palace of the People* (London Borough of Bromley Library Service, 1986)

FACTORIES

Bracegirdle, Brian. *The Archaeology of the Industrial Revolution* (Heinemann, 1973)

Brockman, Harold. *The British Architect in Industry 1841–1940* (George Allen & Unwin, 1974)

Buchanan, R. A. *Industrial Archaeology in Britain* (Penguin Books, 1972)

Burton, Anthony. *The National Trust Guide to Our Industrial Past* (George Philip, 1983)

Jones, Edgar. *Industrial Architecture in Britain 1750–1939* (Batsford, 1985)

Pierson, W. H. Jr 'Notes on an Early Industrial Architecture in England', *Journal of the Society of Architectural Historians (USA)* (volume 8, numbers 1–2, January–June 1949)

Raistrick, Arthur. *Industrial Archaeology: an Historical Survey* (Eyre Methuen, 1972)

Smith, David M. *The Industrial Archaeology of the East Midlands* (David & Charles/Macdonald, 1965)

Sundstrom, Eric. *Work Places* (Cambridge University Press, 1986)

FORTRESSES AND MILITARY BUILDINGS

Ashdown, Charles H. *British Castles* (Adam & Charles Black, 1911)

Fry, P. S. *The David & Charles Book of Castles* (David & Charles, 1980)

Hughes, Quentin. *Military Architecture* (Hugh Evelyn, 1974)

Kightley, Charles. *Strongholds of the Realm* (Thames & Hudson, 1979)

Mears, Kenneth J. *The Tower of London: 900 Years of English History* (Phaidon, 1988)

Renn, D. F. *Norman Castles in Britain* (London, John Baker; New York, Humanities Press, 1968)

Thompson, A. Hamilton. *Military Architecture in England during the Middle Ages* (Oxford University Press, 1912)

BIBLIOGRAPHY

GOVERNMENT BUILDINGS

Colvin, H. M. (general editor). *History of the King's Works* (HMSO, 1963ff)

Toplis, Ian. *The Foreign Office: an Architectural History* (Mansell Publishing, 1987)

HOSPITALS

Clay, Rotha Mary. *The Mediaeval Hospitals of England* (Methuen, 1909)

Forty, Adrian. 'The Modern Hospital in England and France: the Social and Medical Uses of Architecture' in *Buildings and Society* (edited by Anthony D. King; see **General** section)

Hobson, J. M. *Some Early and Later Houses of Pity* (Routledge, 1926)

King, Anthony. 'Hospital Planning: Revised Thoughts on the Origin of the Pavilion Principle in England', *Medical History* (volume 10, 1966)

Leistikow, Dankwort. *Ten Centuries of European Hospital Architecture* (C. H. Boeringer Sohn, Ingelheim an Rhein, 1967)

Medvei, V. and Thornton, J. (editors). *The Royal Hospital of St Bartholomew 1123–1973* (Royal Hospital of St Bartholomew, London, 1974)

Nuttgens, Patrick. *York: the Continuing City* (Faber & Faber, 1976)

Thompson, John D. and Goldin, Grace. *The Hospital, a Social and Architectural History* (Yale University Press, 1975)

INNS, HOTELS AND RESTAURANTS

Burke, Thomas. *English Inns* (Collins, 1944)

Richardson, A. E. *The Old Inns of England* (Batsford, 1934)

Taylor, Derek and Bush, David. *The Golden Age of British Hotels* (Northwood, 1974)

Thorne, Robert. 'Places of Refreshment in the Nineteenth-Century City' in *Buildings and Society* (edited by Anthony D. King; see **General** section)

LIBRARIES

Clark, J. W. *The Care of Books* (Cambridge University Press, second edition 1909)

Kelly, Thomas. *A History of Public Libraries in Great Britain 1845–1975* (Library Association, 1977)

Kelly, Thomas. *Books for the People: an illustrated history of the British public library* (André Deutsch, 1977)

Kelly, Thomas. *Early Public Libraries: a history of the public library in Great Britain before 1850* (Library Association, 1966)

Streeter, Burnett Hillman. *The Chained Library* (Macmillan, 1931)

Thompson, Anthony. *Library Buildings of Britain and Europe* (Butterworth, 1963)

MARKETS

Archer, Ian, Barron, Caroline and Harding, Vanessa. *Hugh Alley's Caveat: the markets of London in 1598* (London Topographical Society, 1988)

Hillman, Judy. *The Rebirth of Covent Garden* (GLC, 1986)

Thorne, Robert. *Covent Garden Market, its History and Restoration* (Architectural Press, 1980)

MUSEUMS

Crook, Dr J. Mordaunt. *The British Museum* (Allen Lane, The Penguin Press, 1972)

Hudson, Kenneth and Nicholls, Ann. *The Cambridge Guide to the Museums of Britain and Ireland* (Cambridge University Press, 1987)

Impey, Oliver and MacGregor, Arthur. *The Origins of Museums* (Oxford University Press, 1985)

Simcock, A. V. *The Ashmolean Museum and Oxford Science 1683–1983* (Museum of the History of Science, Oxford, 1984)

Thompson, John. *Manual of Curatorship* (Butterworths/Museums Association, 1986)

OFFICES

Catchpole, Tim. *London Skylines* (London Research Centre, 1987)

Cowan, Peter et al. *The Office: a Facet of Urban Growth* (Heinemann, 1969)

Hoare, Henry P. R. *Hoare's Bank: a record 1673–1932* (C. Hoare & Co, 1932)

Lubbock, Peter J. A. *The Halls of the Livery Companies of the City of London* (Published under the Patronage of Jones Lang Wootton, London, 1981)

Marber, Paul and Marber, Paula (editors). *Office Development* (Estates Gazette Publications, 1985)

PALACES

Adair, John. *The Royal Palaces of Britain* (Thames & Hudson, 1981)

Charlton, John. *The Banqueting House, Whitehall* (Department of the Environment, 1983)

Cox, Montagu H. and Norman, Philip (general editors). *Survey of London, volumes XIII and XIV* (London County Council, 1930/1)

Fawcett, Richard. *The Palace of Holyrood House* (HMSO, 1988)

McKean, Charles. *Edinburgh: an illustrated architectural guide* (RIAS and Scottish Academic Press, 1983)

Robinson, John Martin. *Royal Residences* (Macdonald, 1982)

Williams, Neville. *Royal Homes of Great Britain from Mediaeval to Modern Times* (Lutterworth Press, 1971)

Williams, Neville. *The Royal Residences of Great Britain* (Barrie & Rockliff, 1960)

PARLIAMENT HOUSES

Cormack, Patrick. *Westminster Palace and People* (Warne, 1981)

Jones, Christopher. *The Great Palace* (BBC, 1983)

Kinvig, R. H. *The Isle of Man: a social, cultural and political history* (Liverpool University Press, 1975)

McKean, Charles. op cit under **Palaces**

BIBLIOGRAPHY

PLACES OF WORSHIP

Barnett, Richard D. and Levy, Abraham. *The Bevis Marks Synagogue* (Society of Heshaim, 1970)

Fenwick, Hubert. *Scotland's Abbeys and Cathedrals* (Robert Hale, 1978)

Rodwell, Warwick and Bentley, James. *Our Christian Heritage* (George Philip, 1984)

Royal Commission on the Ancient and Historical Monuments of Scotland. *Galloway, volume 1, Wigtown* (HMSO, 1912); and *Argyll, volume 4, Iona* (HMSO, 1982)

Sparks, Margaret (editor). *The Parish of St Martin and St Paul, Canterbury: historical essays in memory of James Hobbs* (The Friends of St Martin's, Canterbury, 1980)

POST OFFICES

Farrugia, Jean. *The Life and Work of Sir Rowland Hill* (National Postal Museum, 1979)

Farrugia, Jean and Gammons, Tony. *Carrying British Mails* (National Postal Museum, 1980)

Gammons, Tony. *The Early Days of the Postal Service* (National Postal Museum, 1986)

Post Office Archives. *Historical Summaries nos 5, 9 and 16* (Published by Post Office Archives)

Rider, Bevan. *Bristol First* (Bristol & West Building Society, 1984)

POWER STATIONS

Cochrane, Rob. *Cradle of Power: the Story of the Deptford Power Stations* (Central Electricity Generating Board, South Eastern Region, 1985)

Cochrane, Rob. *Power to the People: the Story of the National Grid* (Newnes, 1985)

PRISONS

Fairweather, Leslie. 'Prison Architecture in England', *British Journal of Criminology* (volume 4, April 1961)

Howard, D. L. *The English Prisons: Their Past and Their Future* (Methuen, 1960)

Johnston, Norman. *The Human Cage: a Brief History of Prison Architecture* (Walker & Co, New York, 1973)

Pugh, Ralph. *Imprisonment in Mediaeval England* (Cambridge University Press, 1968)

Tomlinson, Heather. 'Design and Reform: the "Separate System" in the Nineteenth Century English Prison' in *Buildings and Society* (edited by Anthony D. King; see **General** section)

RAILWAY STATIONS

Andrews, Cyril B. *The Railway Age* (Country Life, 1937)

Barman, Christian. *An Introduction to Railway Architecture* (Art and Technics, London, 1950)

Betjeman, John. *London's Historic Railway Stations* (John Murray, 1972)

BIBLIOGRAPHY

Biddle, Gordon. *Great Railway Stations of Britain* (David & Charles, 1986)

Biddle, Gordon and Spence, J. *The British Railway Station* (David & Charles, 1977)

Binney, Marcus and Pearce, David (editors). *Railway Architecture* (Orbis, 1979)

Fitzgerald, R. S. *Liverpool Road, Manchester: an Historical and Architectural Survey* (Manchester University Press, 1980)

Jackson, Alan A. *London's Metropolitan Railway* (David & Charles, 1986)

Jackson, Alan A. *London's Termini* (David & Charles, 1985)

Johnston, Colin and Hume, John R. *Glasgow's Underground* (David & Charles, 1979)

Makepeace, Chris (editor). *Oldest in the World: the story of Liverpool Road Station, Manchester, 1830–1980* (Liverpool Road Station Society & Manchester Region Industrial Archaeology Society)

Richards, Jeffrey and Mackenzie, John M. *The Railway Station: a Social History* (Oxford University Press, 1986)

SHOPPING ARCADES AND MALLS

Adburgham, Alison. *Shops & Shopping 1800–1914* (George Allen & Unwin, 1981)

Artley, Alexandra. *The Golden Age of Shop Design* (Architectural Press, 1975)

Beddington, Nadine. *Design for Shopping Centres* (Butterworth, 1982)

Collison, Barbara. *Kendals: one hundred and fifty years 1836–1986* (Kendals, Manchester, 1986)

Jeffreys, J. B. *Retail Trading in Britain 1850–1950* (Cambridge University Press, 1954)

MacKeith, Margaret. *Shopping Arcades 1817–1939* (Mansell, 1985)

MacKeith, Margaret. *The History and Conservation of Shopping Arcades* (Mansell, 1986)

MacKeith, Margaret. 'Cathedrals of Commerce', in *Heritage* (vol 1 no 2 1984, pp54–6)

Somake, Ellis and Hellberg, Rolf. *Shops and Stores Today* (Batsford, 1956)

TELEPHONY BUILDINGS

Baldwin, F. G. C. *The History of the Telephone in the United Kingdom* (Chapman & Hall, 1938)

Britain's Public Payphones: a social history (British Telecommunications plc, 1984)

THEATRES

Chambers, E. *The Elizabethan Stage* (Oxford University Press, 1913)

Chambers, E. *The Mediaeval Stage* (Oxford University Press, 1903)

Leacroft, Helen and Richard. *Theatre & Playhouse* (Methuen, 1984)

Leacroft, Richard. *Development of the English Playhouse* (Eyre Methuen, 1973)

Mackintosh, Iain and Sell, Michael. *Curtains!!!* (John Offord [Publications] Ltd, 1982)

Moro, Peter and Little, Bryan. *The Story of the Theatre Royal, Bristol* (Trustees of the Theatre Royal, 1981)

Mullin, Donald C. *The Development of the Playhouse* (University of California Press, 1970)

Nicoll, Allardyce. *The English Theatre* (Nelson, 1936)

ZOOS

Blunt, Wilfred *The Ark in the Park* (Hamish Hamilton, 1976)

Hancocks, David. *Animals and Architecture* (Hugh Evelyn, 1971)

Mitchell, P. Chalmers *Centenary History of the Zoological Society of London* (Zoological Society of London, 1929)

Schomberg, Geoffrey. *The Penguin Guide to British Zoos* (Penguin, 1970)

Vevers, G. *London's Zoo* (Bodley Head, 1976)

ACKNOWLEDGEMENTS

I could not have attempted this book without help from many sources, individuals and organisations. The key books and other published references which I have used are listed in the bibliography; in addition to these, and my editor, Jane Rowe, I wish to acknowledge the help of the following:

Allan Ramsay Library, Biggar; American Multi-Cinema Inc; Arrowcroft Group Ltd; David Attwell; BAT Industries; Nadine Beddington RIBA; Birmingham Central Library; Bristol Old Vic Trust; British Airports Authority; British Broadcasting Corporation; British Library; British Museum; British Rail Property Board; British Telecommunications plc; Building Design Partnership; C. Hoare & Co; Canterbury Central Library; Rodney Carron, partner, Chapman Taylor Partners, architects; Catholic Central Library; Central Electricity Generating Board; Chetham's Library, Manchester; Michael Chrimes, Librarian, Institution of Civil Engineers; Cinema Theatre Association; City of Cardiff; City of Derby Museums & Art Gallery; City of London Corporation; City of London Guildhall Library; Colchester Archaeological Trust Ltd; Council for Places of Worship; Crown Estate Commissioners; Robert Cruse; Dr Colin Cunningham; Fr Kit Cunningham, Rector of St Etheldreda's Catholic Church; Dr Roger Custance, Archivist, Winchester College; Margaret Davies, conservation architect with Cecil Denny Highton, architects; Chris Dean, Archivist, St Paul's School; Donaldsons; Robert Double; English Heritage; Nicholas Fogg; GEC-Marconi Ltd; Georgian Theatre Royal, Richmond; Granada Television Ltd; Greater Manchester Museum of Science & Industry; Guardian Royal Exchange Assurance; The Guild School Association of Stratford-upon-Avon; Hampshire County Council; Vanessa Harding; Harlow & District Sports Trust; Harwich Electric Palace Trust; Hastings Borough Council; Heritage Division, London Borough of Sutton Leisure Services; Home Office; Canon Reginald Humphriss; Canon Derek Ingram Hill of Canterbury Cathedral; Institution of Electrical Engineers; International Shakespeare Globe Centre; Islamic Cultural Centre; Geraint John, Head of Technical Unit for Sport, Sports Council; Ruth Kamen and the staff of the British Architectural Library; Kendals, Manchester; John King; Land Securities Properties Ltd; Leeds City Council; L. G. Mouchel and Partners; Library Association; Liverpool Central Library; Lloyd's of London; London Borough of Bromley Libraries; London Research Centre; Mrs Margaret Magnusson, Corps Library, Institution of Royal Engineers; Chris Makepeace; Manchester Central Library; Charles McKean, Secretary, The Royal Incorporation of Architects in Scotland; Merseyside Development Corporation; Derek Middleton; Midland Hotels Ltd; Museum of the History of Science, Oxford; Museum of London; Museums & Galleries Commission; National Army Museum; National Sports Centre; Olympia & York (Canary

Wharf) Ltd; Richard Owen, British Railways Board Department of Architecture, Design & Environment; Phaidon Press Ltd; The Post Office; Post Office Archives; Property Services Agency; Royal Commission on Historical Monuments (England); Royal Commission on the Ancient and Historical Monuments of Scotland; Royal Incorporation of Architects in Scotland; Royal Institution of Chartered Surveyors; Royal Opera House, Covent Garden; Savoy Group; Selfridges; Professor James A. Smiechen, Department of History, Central Michigan University; Spanish and Portuguese Jews' Congregation; Sports Council; St Katharine-by-the-Tower Ltd; Telecom Technology Showcase; Theatres Trust; Robert Thorne; United International Pictures (UK); Dr Paul Walker; Watts & Partners; West Sussex County Council; James Williams, partner, Drivers Jonas, chartered surveyors; Winchester Research Unit; Geoffrey Yeo, Archivist, St Bartholomew's Hospital; Zoological Society of London.

On a personal basis, I am grateful to the Gunning family of Liverpool, whose hospitality enabled me to make progress on a crucial stage of my research; to Gerard and Margaret Murray for reading my text for historical accuracy; and above all to my more-than-wife Elizabeth, who has kept my constantly amended drafts up to date and preserved my sanity, and to James, Olivia, Edward (Maughold) and Benjamin for seeing less of their father than was their due during the year that this book was in gestation.

Thank you all.

INDEX

Figures in **bold** denote illustrations